Praise for
The Adventurous Couple's Guide to Sex Toys

"No longer are toys solely for solo pleasure. Violet's vast research and expertise in this area can guide both novice and toy-experienced couples."

—Lou Paget, author of *The Great Lover Playbook*

"This how-to presents toys as safe and fun options for heterosexual couples. Blue, author of numerous excellent sex guides from Cleis Press, concisely covers all the usual suspects: vibrators, dildos, plugs, 'toys for boys,' BDSM (bondage & discipline/sadomasochism) gear, how to talk about toys with your partner, and how to use them.... She surveys the wide variety of products very well, with ample safe-sex and safety reminders."

—*Library Journal*

"*The Adventurous Couple's Guide to Sex Toys* shows readers successful ways to introduce sex toys into relationships. This new book continues Blue's focus on cultivating and maintaining the magic between lovers. As the editor of bestselling erotica anthologies especially for couples—*Sweet Life*, *Sweet Life 2*, and *Sweet Danger*—she knows how to bring the heat."

—Good Vibrations

THE **ADVENTUROUS COUPLE'S** GUIDE TO **SEX TOYS**

THE **ADVENTUROUS COUPLE'S** GUIDE TO **SEX TOYS**

VIOLET BLUE

FOREWORD BY CHARLIE GLICKMAN, PhD
ILLUSTRATED BY ZANNE DeJANVIER

Published in the United States by Cleis Press, Inc., 2246 Sixth Street, Berkeley, California 94710.

Printed in the United States.
Cover design: Scott Idleman
Cover photograph: iStockphoto
Text design: Karen Quigg
Second Edition.
10 9 8 7 6 5 4 3 2 1

Trade paper ISBN: 978-1-57344-972-4
E-book ISBN: 978-1-57344-977-9

Library of Congress Cataloging-in-Publication Data is available.

contents

Illustrations

Foreword

Sex toys have changed a lot in the more than twenty years that I've been a sex educator. Back in those days, most of them were made of low-quality materials and it was almost impossible to find good information on how to pick out a toy or how to use it once you had it in your hands. Having to choose between the furtiveness of going into a "dirty" book store and trying to order a toy online, many people felt embarrassed about using "marital aids," and manufacturers knew they didn't need to worry about customer feedback or quality control. After all, if a toy broke, who'd complain?

But even more than that, a lot of toys weren't designed all that well. They had weird bumps or shapes that didn't seem to do anything. Or they were marketed as novelties, as if sexual pleasure wasn't important. A few small companies were trying to offer better products, but not many people knew about them.

There have been some pretty big changes since then. As more people, and especially more women, have spoken publicly about enjoying sex toys, the industry has made some significant shifts. These days, you can find toys in a wide price range, from inexpensive ones that let you explore and experiment without breaking the bank to high-tech gadgets with all sorts of fancy features. New body-safe materials have become available across the industry, offering different alternatives to sex toy designers. And more products than ever before are made by people who understand the anatomy of pleasure and sexual response.

Along with these new directions in the industry, now there's more information about sex toys and how to use them than there used to be. You don't need to figure it all out yourself anymore, which means you can more easily find the gadgets that will give you the pleasure you want. Of course, it can sometimes be hard to figure out which information is worth trusting. Plenty of folks write about sex online, and they don't always agree on the facts. And there are all sorts of urban legends, old information, and bad advice floating around. Fortunately, Violet Blue's *The Adventurous Couple's Guide to Sex Toys* is here to help.

I first met Violet when we worked together at Good Vibrations, the San Francisco Bay Area–based sex-positive sex toy company. She was working in the marketing department and I ran the workshops and education programs, but when it came right down to it, we were doing the same thing: getting sex-positive information out into the world. In many ways, Good Vibrations was the catalyst for a lot of the positive changes in the sex toy industry. The company supported the people who were making better products and writing amazing how-to books, and helped introduce the idea that the world deserved top-notch toys and information. Good Vibrations made it easy and comfortable for people of all genders to discover sex toys, and once the manufacturers realized that there was a market for better products, they got on board.

When Violet and I worked together, we talked a lot about the kinds of information we wanted people to have. After all, nobody is born knowing anything about sex, and we knew how important it was to help folks get the tips and ideas they need to have fun. In the time since then, Violet's many books have become some of my favorites to recommend. They've helped thousands of people explore oral sex, sexual fantasies, porn, and yes, sex toys. You might not realize how much there is to know about toys and other pleasure devices, but as someone who has worked with plenty of people and has trained many sex educators, I can tell you that there's a lot to these devices, and this book has all the information you need to discover your new favorite toy.

If you've never experimented with sex toys, Violet has many great ideas and tips to help you figure out which ones to start with. And if you already have a bedside drawer full of fun stuff, she has tons of suggestions for getting the most out of them and for discovering new pleasures. Plus, there's lots of information about some sex toys you might never have heard of before.

So if you're ready to see for yourself just what fun is waiting for you, let *The Adventurous Couple's Guide to Sex Toys* be your map. I hope you have incredible pleasure and a lot of fun.

Charlie Glickman, PhD

The Right Tools for Fifty Shades of Fun

Fifty Shades of Grey has been inspiring a lot of people to bring a little kinky fun into the bedroom. Whether you want to explore S/M or just add a little heat to your sex life, here's a list of the toys from the book to make your fantasies come true.

Blindfold—Your lover won't know what's coming.

Restraints—Available in fabric or leather, they work better than scarves.

Hitachi Magic Wand vibrator

Vaginal balls—Check out Fun Factory's Smartballs.

Riding crop—Available online at a BDSM store or your local tack shop.

Spreader bar—Hold your lover in place and at your mercy.

Nipple clamps—If your partner likes having their nipples pinched, these keep your hands free for other fun.

Flogger—Whether for fantasy or for impact play, floggers can be lots of fun. Be sure to read up on how to use one.

Butt plug—Anal play can be a great add-on to sex or it can be the main course. Do a little research to make sure you do it right.

Exploring S/M is a lot more fun when you have a little know-how. Get a copy of Violet's book *The Ultimate Guide to Sexual Fantasy* for lots of great ideas for playing with your desires. Tristan Taormino's *The Ultimate Guide to Kink* offers all the tips you need to make it safe, fun, and hot!

—CG

Chapter 1

Basic Models, and Care and Feeding of Your Toys

If we approached the world of sex toys as a scientist might, classifying toys by purpose, species, and effectiveness, we might go a very long time until our next orgasm. Sure, in its broadest definition, anything can be a *sex toy*—because any object, image, or thing used for erotic stimulation could legitimately be called a sex toy. But an object's erotic potential lies in the eye of the beholder. Toys and novelties made for the express purpose of sexual gratification are a wild and woolly category of creatures, ranging from the practical and reliable to the outrageous, silly, sometimes dangerous, and occasionally deliciously decadent.

While sex toys have been around for centuries, appreciating the modern selection of toys you can find online and in your local sex shops requires only a minimal understanding of recent developments in sex toy evolution.

Plainly put, there are *novelties*...and then there are toys made for sex. Confused? Most sex toys that you'll find in garden-variety retail sex toy stores are created, marketed, and sold "for novelty use only," meaning that while the toy companies explicitly know that people are using their toys for sex, they sell them categorized as novelties. Why they do this is anyone's guess; perhaps it's so they can avoid responsibility for faulty merchandise, as many sex toys are made poorly (almost all novelty sex toys are made cheaply in Chinese factories), or perhaps it's so they can make outrageous claims on the packaging and marketing materials; in some U.S. states where sex toys are against the law to sell, distribute, or own, this may also be a way to circumvent legalities about products intended for sexual gratification.

Novelty sex toys are the most widely available, as they have a virtual stranglehold on American distribution, and they are the least expensive. In practical terms, this is not such a bad thing. You'll find the widest selection and best prices in the novelty toy market, making these toys a great way to try new things without breaking the bank; to get a certain size, shape, or functionality you desire; or to find that exact shade of pink you prefer. Novelties often feature the latest innovations in design and use—but also tend to break easily. Some are made with noxious materials, and some are shipped already defective but with user-unfriendly return policies. Technically speaking, novelties aren't made for sex, though they can conjure up an orgasm pretty well. Identifying these toys in stores is easy, as they have the most polished or garish (and sometimes offensive) packaging, the phrase "for novelty use" is printed somewhere on the package, and they typically come from companies such as Doc Johnson, Vibratex, Pipedream, or Adam and Eve. In any case, it's always "buyer beware" when you purchase a sex toy, and nowhere else is it more essential for you as consumer to be prepared with knowledge about the products, even before plunking down a few bucks on a plastic discount vibrator.

Not all sex toys are sold as novelties. Toys marketed as sex toys come from independent manufacturers and are created with the consumer's pleasure as their express purpose. A growing number of high-quality sex toy companies do business in the United States and in the U.K., and many seem to prize sexual health and pleasure as the key building blocks of both their businesses and their products. Many of these companies are women-owned, though many have not yet broken into the "old boys' network" of distribution to novelty stores. You can find products—or rather, "pleasure instruments"—from Tantus, Vixen Creations, Fun Factory, and Sportsheets mostly online and in "women-friendly" stores and sex toy boutiques that hand-pick their product selections. These companies have raised the bar on what people expect when they plunk down their hard-earned cash for something nice to shove up their asses.

So there are novelties, and there are sex toys, or "pleasure instruments," and you can expect to find many of both types displayed side-by-side at reputable retailers. Sometimes you'll even see novelty toy manufacturers making products that are similar to sex toys; the decision to buy a novelty (or not) is simply a question of quality, price, and convenience. Know what you're looking for, and what you'll likely encounter online and in stores, and you'll be a smart customer—and, in the end, a satisfied one.

Vibrators

Nowhere is the world of sex toys more exciting and diverse than with vibrators. It's safe to say that if you can imagine it, someone somewhere has made a vibrator out of it. You can find vibrators that mount on your tongue or fit on the end of your finger, or resemble whimsical waterproof rubber duckies, and even penises.

It's safe to say that the most iconic vibrator is the rocket-shaped Slimline vibe. It's the model that most people imagine when they think of the word *vibrator*. It's been featured since the 1970s in magazine back page ads for "massagers" and in countless porn films. And it's a classic for a reason: It's a really solid vibrator, still outselling its younger, more modern counterparts.

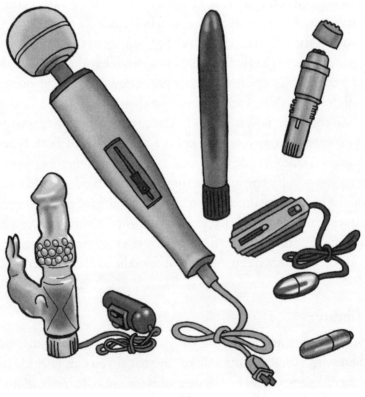

Illus. 1: Vibrators

Batteries and Vibrators

Battery-powered vibes typically run on AA, AAA, C, or watch batteries. For stronger vibrations, pop in fresh batteries; already-used ones provide a lighter buzz. Always wash your hands after handling batteries. To prolong the life of vibrator and batteries, remove the batteries when not in use. Double that precaution before an airplane trip; no one wants an accidentally turned-on vibe buzzing in their suitcase when navigating the airport security lines.

The Slimline is a plastic cylinder with a narrow tip; it comes in a variety of sizes, from keychain-sized to 9 inches long, and it typically has a variable-speed dial. Made of hard plastic, it's terrific for external stimulation or firm internal penetration, and it tends to have a healthy lifespan. You'll be glad to know that hard plastic vibes amplify vibration, making them stronger vibrators than their rubber- or silicone-encased counterparts, whose softer materials absorb vibration.

Another common vibrator is the egg, or bullet, vibe. These look just like their namesakes and usually have a cord trailing out of one end attached to a controller containing the batteries and the on/off (or adjustable) power switch. These are primarily vibes only for external use, meant for clitoral stimulation. Some people do insert these, though it's not recommended because pulling on the cord (like a tampon) for retrieval is a shaky situation with these cheaply made vibes, since the cord may unexpectedly detach form the bullet, leaving it inside. Some bullet vibes have advanced controllers with programmable microchips, and, while on the pricey side, they're worth it for the extremely arousing range of pulses, beats, variations, and roller-coaster effects that they deliver.

Hand-held vibes come in varieties too numerous to list here, but models of interest include the Pocket Rocket, the Hitachi Magic Wand, the Tongue, and the ergonomic Natural Contours. The Pocket Rocket is a simple, one-speed, finger-sized external vibe marketed for acupressure; it fits neatly in a purse or pocket (hence the name). Electric Hitachi Magic Wands are considered the strongest vibrators available; their tennis-ball head nestles nicely between the thighs for blissful external stimulation, and some sex toy companies have created attachments to give the Hitachi an insertable extension. The Tongue frankly looks like a chicken cutlet, but it's a battery-powered, adjustable-speed vibe made to mimic a tongue performing oral sex. And the woman-created Natural Contours line of hand-held battery vibes come in a range of styles and shapes, fit nicely into the shape of your hand, and look more like plastic art objects than vibrators.

Ever heard of the "rabbit"? Made famous on an episode of the TV show *Sex and the City* in which character Charlotte disappears for days on end with her new vibrator, these dual-action (or "twice as nice") vibes are very popular, indeed. They combine a shaft for penetration with another buzzy little vibe at the base (usually in the shape of an animal, like a bunny), well situated for clitoral stimulation during penetration. Often, the shaft will have an internal ring of "pearls"—small plastic beads that undulate to massage the vaginal barrel when the shaft is activated. Typically, the shaft rotates in a gyrating fashion while the clit vibe vibrates, though usually each of these functions is independent of one another and the user can choose to use one or the other, or both, and at whatever speed or intensity she prefers. It's no surprise that these toys have legions of loyal followers, for they combine the perfect types of stimulation that help the user come (and come fast!) during penetration.

Dual-action vibes like this are available in hundreds of shapes, sizes, styles, and varieties. The main differences lie in the length, shape, and girth of the shaft, and in the size of the clit stimulator and its distance from the shaft. Sometimes selection can be tricky, as no two women's clits are exactly the same distance from their vaginal opening. Advanced dual-action vibes have microchip controllers, allowing the user to figure out as many ways as possible that she can come with a variety of programmable pulses, shudders, shakes, vibrations, and more. These toys are also suitable for quite enjoyable anal experimentation, as the clit vibe at the base serves as both a stopping point for safe anal insertion and a delicious buzz for the vaginal opening or testicles.

Originally manufactured in Japan where genital representation on sex toys was once illegal, today's dual-action vibes usually sport smiling little samurai faces on the shaft, and any number of tiny animal companions at the base—rabbit, beaver, bird, even platypus. The tradition is still in practice, even with the cheap imitations now coming out of China, but if you decide that this vibe fits nicely into your orgasmic arsenal, do spend a bit more to get a Japanese-made version, as it will be better made and last longer than its cloned Chinese and American counterparts. But beware of sex toy companies making the marketing claim that they have "the original rabbit"; it may not be true.

The category of vibrators worn on the finger will be of special interest throughout this book, as most finger vibes are

---

Keep It Clean

Once a toy, finger, or penis has touched an anus (whether your own
or someone else's), don't let it come in contact with your vulva or
vagina—no matter what you've seen in porn. The anus is host to bacteria that cause vaginal infections, no matter how recent the shower.
Don't let tonight's love fest turn into tomorrow's infection; use a
condom or glove to create a clean surface when moving from anus
to vagina (though vagina to anus is fine). And you'd better *bet* that
those porn stars get infections just like the rest of us.

---

discreet enough to be slipped on during foreplay or sex to make
those fingers do double time when they explore your lover's nipples, clit, penis, or outer part of the anus. Finger vibes come in
a variety of permutations, but the most common version you'll
see is the awkwardly named Fukuoku. This hard plastic,
watch-battery-powered vibe slips onto the end of a finger, runs
at one speed, and comes with a variety of thin, textured silicone sheaths. But oodles of finger vibe versions are available,
from little tickly outer space creatures to finger bullets, complete with external battery packs providing controllers with
variable (and programmable) speeds and functions. Also of note
are "tongue vibes," which strap to one's tongue for use in oral
sex (see chapter 3, Come Together).

Dildos

A dildo is basically defined as any penetrative, nonvibrating
device—but aside from the clinical definition of what makes a dildo
not a vibrator, dildos comprise a vast category of wonderful,

whimsical, bizarre, and sometimes-scary penetration toys. Dildos are used mostly for vaginal and anal penetration, though they can also be used for wonderfully intense mock blow jobs, especially when worn in a strap-on harness.

In general, dildos come in two styles: representational and nonrepresentational. *Representational* is a loose term here, as even the most realistic dildos tend to look like bizarrely colored doll parts, though the dildo manufacturing industry has created some amazing innovations in body-part realism—most notably with

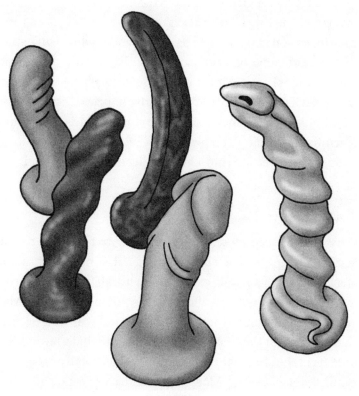

Illus. 2: Dildos

Vixen Creation's incredibly real-feeling silicone Tex dildo (made with VixSkin). Representational dildos typically look like penises in shape, whereas the nonrepresentational models can be anything from smooth shafts in pearlescent turquoise, to mermaids, to bumpy, sculpted figurative works of art.

Some dildos have a suction cup base, allowing the user to stick them on smooth surfaces like bathroom tile or a tub, or even a hard barstool. Dildos made for harness use have a flared, flat base so they fit into the harness base; these dildos are also suitable for safe anal use as the flared base can be used as a handle to retrieve the toy. They're also great for practicing deep throat fellatio, as you can use the base as a handle while you explore the comfort zone of your gag reflex. Extra-long dildos (and double dildos) are great for when you need a little extra reach, when you have mobility issues or wrist injuries, or when a long handle just makes penetration more comfortable. Or, of course, when you like *really* deep penetration. Read more about double dildos in chapter 5, Strap-Ons and Bend Over Boyfriend.

Toys for Boys

We've been gulled by sex toy advertising to think sex toys are just for girls—but that's hardly the case. Use of sex toys among men is far from rare. Men can (and do) use all the toys described in this chapter—not just those in this "for men" section. Many guys love vibration in their genital area and will seek out cup-shaped vibes for the head of the penis, or will find a few exciting options in the above vibrator sections—like hand massage with a bullet vibe in his fist. Men, of course, have prostate glands, so they can enjoy anal stimulation (if they're comfortable with it).

They can adopt a few ideas from the sections on dildos and butt toys in this chapter, and later in chapter 5, Strap-Ons and Bend Over, Boyfriend, they can browse all kinds of info, suggestions, and tips for pleasant prostate play. Lots of men like to have their nipples stimulated and might like to check out the sections on nipple clamps in chapter 4, Kinky Toys for Two. But generally, when you look in the men's sections in hetero retail sex toy sites and in stores, you'll be seeing a lot of cock rings and masturbation sleeves, with no marketing aimed at prostate play. Conversely, in gay stores you'll see butt toys marketed to men, which is sometimes a misnomer, as not all gay men like anal penetration.

Illus. 3: Toys for Boys

A cock ring is a ring worn around the penis and testicles to apply a steady pressure around the base, slightly restricting the blood flow out of the penis after it's engorged. Not for all (but enjoyed by many), a cock ring provides a continuous squeeze to a man's penis and testicles that can make any stimulation feel more pleasurable. It goes over the top of the penis's base and continues around and under the testicles. Cock rings don't help with erectile difficulties, but many men say they help their erections last longer—though the results are different for everyone. But cock rings do have a nice way of pushing everything out and up...making for a nice visual package.

Unless you're experienced with cock rings, never use ones that are metal or aren't stretchy enough to remove easily. These rings can come off only upon ejaculation or when the erection subsides, which means a guy has to ice everything down (to get the blood to retreat from his genitals) if he panics or experiences pain or discomfort. Needless to say, if he experiences pain or discomfort when using a cock ring, he should remove the ring immediately. Cock rings are easiest to apply and remove on men who trim or shave their pubic hair, but that's not required. Just keep an eye on hair that can get snagged when removing a stretchy rubber ring.

Male masturbation sleeves are a category with so many styles, shapes, and models that it would be impossible to list them all here—the world is truly a really big place. From shiny jelly rubber "cock socks" to vibrating pumps and disembodied casts of porn stars, they're all here. The sleeves tend to either be really thoughtfully designed, such as the soft and tight Fleshlight, or be loose and annoying "one-size-fits-some" rubber mouths, and more. What a guy wants when it comes to a masturbation sleeve is entirely up to his fantasy and what he might like to look at when he masturbates; most men don't care what it looks like, because they're either watching porn or running their own fantasy in their heads anyway, and the sleeve does little more than provide sensation that's different than their own hand— making these toys a nice change from the same-old, same-old style of masturbation.

Butt Plugs and Anal Beads

Typically, butt plugs are nonvibrating, bullet-shaped toys, with a flat, flared base, made to insert in the anus during different kinds of sex play, and are intended to stay put. Yet this isn't always what happens—smaller plugs, when properly lubed up for insertion, tend to come out (or shoot out) when the involuntary muscles of the anal sphincter contract and relax, especially at the point of orgasm. Most butt plugs are created in the proper shape to stay put; their wide base and narrow "neck" make them ideal toys for hands-free anal penetration, and they give a lasting feeling of fullness during other activities, such as oral sex, penetration, or hand jobs. Because they're made to stay in place, anal plugs with a narrow neck and bulbous top aren't great for in-and-out thrusting, as the stress of opening and closing the anal muscles tends to feel uncomfortable, especially for those who are sensitive to anal pain.

Sex toys safe for anal penetration have a flared base. That prevents them from being pulled into the anal canal, where they can get lost—a nightmare waiting to happen. The sphincter muscles squeeze and contract involuntarily; we can't control them. This serves to push and pull things in and out of the anus, and once something gets pulled in, there's no guarantee you're going to get it out without a trip to the hospital—which is what you'd have to take to prevent serous injury if, say, a hot, battery-powered vibrator went AWOL. Take a look at a standard butt plug and you'll see exactly what a flared base should look like. Not all toys sold for anal use are actually safe to put in your butt, so please be a sex-smart shopper.

Anal beads are basically a knotted string with plastic beads every inch or so, with a large ring at the end that functions as a handle. Not all anal beads are created equal, and quality ranges

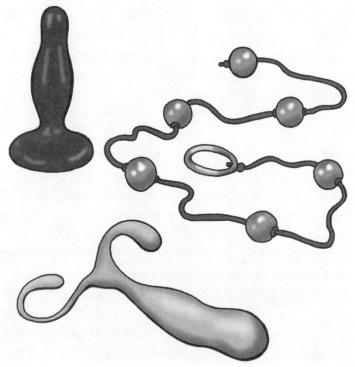

Illus. 3: Butt Plugs and Anal Beads

from cheap plastic to metal and even precious gems. Some versions are beaded wands, rather than strings. Like all butt toys, anal beads should be carefully examined before use. If using the string version, make sure all the knots are secure. Plastic beads are made in factories and the beads themselves often have sharp seams—file down any ridge seams with a nail file to ensure a smooth set of beads. Make sure your handle is secure, and check the base of any "stringless" varieties for strength.

The Aneros (from malegspot.com) is a beautiful white anal plug made specifically for prostate massage. Unlike most plugs for guys, the Aneros was painstakingly researched to come up with the very best design for easy insertion and hands-free prostate massage. The thinking behind its anatomically correct design is that contraction of the sphincter muscles provides the rhythm for orgasmic release, and its creators claim that men can reach multiple orgasms when using their toy correctly. The Aneros ships in a variety of sizes. Whether or not claims of male multiples are true, the Aneros has a loyal following and is a darling of the sex toy boutique scene.

Sex Toy Materials

There's no doubt: What a toy is made of makes all the difference in the world. Most commercially available sex toys are fashioned out of hard plastic, jelly rubber, silicone, vinyl, or softskin (aka Cyberskin or Futurotic). But you'll need to know the two basic differences when choosing a toy: porous versus nonporous materials.

Nonporous toys are made of materials (like silicone, hard plastic, glass, metal, or stone) that are easy to clean and don't retain bacteria in the tiny pockets or pores in the surface. This means that when you clean one of these toys, they're completely clean and don't have the potential to carry STDs or bacteria that can infect (or reinfect) the user. Plastic, glass and Pyrex, metal, and stone sex toys can have their surfaces rendered sterile by washing with unscented antibacterial soap (like Hibiclens) or a solution of 1:10 bleach and water (1:10 rubbing alcohol and water is a fine alternative).

Many consider silicone the perfect sex toy material. Of course, the popularity of silicone toys caused the ethics-free segments of the sex toy industry to start incorrectly labeling jelly rubber toys as silicone (or sili-gel) to hike sales—again, buyer beware. Private companies make silicone toys from medical-grade silicone, so you should never be able to see through a silicone toy; real silicone is *always* opaque. The surface is 100 percent pore-free and silky-smooth, ranging from very firm to floppy-soft, and silicone warms quickly to body temperature and retains its heat for a long time. Silicone toys can be boiled for up to 5 minutes or run in the top rack of the dishwasher for complete sterilization, which is especially awesome for anal toys. Some silicone toys react badly to silicone lubricants, so it's best to use water-based lubes with your silicone toys.

Most sex toys are made of a material usually referred to as jelly rubber, though you'll also see variations like jel-lee, latex jelly, or derivatives like glow-in-the-dark and "realistic" materials such as softskin, Cyberskin, or Futurotic. Jelly rubber toys are very colorful, clear (though not always), shiny, and visually appealing. They're fashioned out of the ultimate "mystery material," mass-produced mostly in Chinese chemical factories with so many mixtures and versions of the material that it's difficult to pin down a set of manufacturer's ingredients. What *is* known, however, is that these materials contain latex, give off a highly chemical smell, leach oils and can leave spots on fabrics and wood, and have a surface that breaks down over time. Softskin, Cyberskin, and Futurotic toys are especially strange; while they feel amazingly real, they react bizarrely with other jelly rubber toys and actually melt into wet puddles of chemical goo on contact—needless to say, don't store these two materials side-by-side. Softskin is the most porous toy of all, able to absorb color from lipstick and even text from newsprint.

No one knows for sure how safe these toys are for internal use; remember, we're talking about the novelty industry, so we can surmise that it'll be about 800 years before clinical tests are done on the long-term effects of jelly rubber chemicals on the cervix and lower colon. Some people have no problems with jelly rubber toys at all and have used them for years uneventfully (except for the orgasm part, which is certainly an event worth talking about). Others have had serious reactions to the latex, or to other unknown chemicals, ranging from anaphylactic shock from latex allergy to recurring infections. On the Web you'll find a plethora of writings about the possible harmful and carcinogenic nature of these toys.

Which is why many sex toy boutiques (as well as this book) recommend that you use a condom on *every* jelly rubber or soft-skin toy that enters your body. If you have no reaction to jelly rubber, and most people don't, remember to keep the toy scrupulously clean. Wash such toys with unscented antibacterial soap (like Hibiclens) or a solution of 1:10 bleach and water (alcohol and water also works fine). Waterproof toys are wonderful in this regard, as they can be completely submerged during cleaning.

Consider porous toys disposable, and once a toy has been used for anal play, make it an anal-only toy. Keep an eye on the surface; once it becomes dull, it's starting to break down and you can never be sure you're getting it clean; so be safe, toss it out, and get a new one. And hey—doesn't everyone want an excuse to go sex toy shopping?

Look for the "Phthalate-Free" Label

For many years, most toy manufacturers used phthalates (pronounced THAL-ates) in their products because these chemicals can make plastic and PVC soft and bendable. While a flexible, softer texture is ideal for sex toys, it turns out that phthalates aren't so hot.

In 2001, toy makers began hearing reports that phthalates might not be safe because they could be absorbed by mucous membranes and cause health problems. Unfortunately, there's been very little research about how this might affect sex toys, but just to be safe, most manufacturers stopped using these ingredients in their toys. As a result, you might see a "phthalate-free" label on the packaging.

Phthalates are mostly used in plastic, jelly rubber, and PVC toys, so silicone, glass, and metal sex toys have always been phthalate-free. If you're concerned about this issue, stick with these materials and you'll be all set.

—CG

Chapter 2

First-Time Toys and Gifts

Want to give your special someone a sex toy? Nothing says "sexy" like giving a sex toy to a lover or potential lover. Imagine the blushing look of wicked delight on her face when she unwraps a box containing a very special sex toy— a simple gesture that conveys how sexy you think she is, and hints at all the things you'd like to do with her. Better yet, think about how giving your guy a butt plug reveals that much more about the naughty thoughts you're having, and how you'd like nothing less than to turn those thoughts into erotic reality. Getting and giving sex toy presents is a huge turn-on. It's the biggest signifier that hot sex is right around the corner— and all that one of you has to do is unwrap that package. Unwrapping each other's "packages" will follow, in short order, I promise you.

Buying someone an intimate gift isn't like grabbing a last-minute bouquet of flowers from the corner store on Valentine's Day. In addition to the overwhelming amount of choices, health considerations, and infinite fantasy possibilities that you can unlock with sex toys for two, you also have many titillating decisions to make when it comes to choosing or assembling the perfect sex toy present.

And believe me, working in sex toy retailing for nearly eight years had me counseling literally hundreds of such "impulse buy" shoppers. These shoppers had a lot more to consider than just what color to choose and what was the most popular vibrator style that season. Their reactions have helped me compile some possibilities for you to consider before clicking your mouse on the "buy" button or swoop into the local sex toy retailer for a naughty-but-nice present. Above all, don't forget to make a shopping checklist before you buy.

The Sex Toy Novice

Is your lover new to sex toys? Want to surprise him or her with a little something sexy for a special occasion? This is such a fun situation to find yourself in: A whole world of sex toys and choices awaits, and your lover gets to try out a toy for the very first time, sharing the experience with you. Nothing could be hotter, sexier, or more intimate.

Will your gift be a surprise? While slow seductions and planned fantasies are among life's exquisite pleasures, giving your sweetie something you know they're not expecting—but want— makes for an unforgettable sexual tryst. Yet if it's too unexpected, you might be met with shock, or worse. Make sure he or she has some idea that something hot's coming. Presenting someone with a sex toy when they're having a bad day, feel exhausted, or wish they'd showered before seeing you might make them feel awk-ward, or pressured. Plan ahead for a successful "reveal," and make sure you've had some indication that they'd like to get frisky with you—*and* with the novelty of a sex toy.

If you don't talk with each other about sex or haven't even broached the topic, a sex toy might not be the right way to get the conversation started. In fact, if the idea of sex toys is totally new to your lover and you give them a bright pink buzzing bunny, it might startle them so much that it closes a door in your relationship for some time to come. Make sure you know they're even remotely interested in sexual play or experimen‑ tation beforehand, by chatting about it. You don't need to give away your surprise or plans for seduction, but do lightly check in with him or her about trying something new in bed, just the two of you—this way, you can fish around for anything that might be potentially "off the list" so that you don't wind up being a "bad Santa."

If you want to surprise your honey with a sex toy present that takes you out of your sexual routines (or a rut), you're going to have to be the one to start talking about it. This will be easy if you talk about sex and experimentation regularly in your rela‑ tionship, though a bit daunting if you never talk about sex but just do it. Telling him or her that you want to try something new sexually can feel stressful—and if it's motivated by a secret

---

Initiating Your First Sex Toy Conversation

Watch a movie with a sex toy scene in it, so you can comment on it later; try *Better Than Chocolate*, *The Slums of Beverly Hills*, or *But I'm a Cheerleader*.

Mention that you saw a news item about sex toys and comment on the situation: Search Google News with "sex toys" as your query, to get a bevy of recent results.

fantasy, this is an understatement. In fact, even *thinking* about talking about sex is stressful sometimes! If you've never brought up the subject of sex with your partner, don't worry. If you have what you consider a routine style of sex, telling your partner that you want something to change is scary, and starting a conversation about your desires to sexually experiment can make you feel vulnerable. This is as true with familiar sexual fantasies that predate your relationship as it is with new fantasies you discover as time goes by. Opening yourself up and asking for something you want sexually takes courage—but it also gives you an opportunity to learn more about what your lover likes and dislikes.

If you're the one bringing it up, reverse roles for a minute: If you don't normally talk about sex in your relationship and then suddenly one of you wants to, it might be upsetting—at first. Your lover may wonder if you've been withholding sexual secrets all along. But it's very likely that your opening up to them will give your lover the opportunity to tell you what's on their mind about sex, too.

Her First Vibrator (or Butt Plug, G-Spot Toy, Etc.)

Okay, enough talk about talking. You're both ready to take the plunge into sex toy play, and you're not worried about how your daring device will be received—but you do want to make sure that it's the right toy. Be sure to read through chapter 1, Basic Models, and Care and Feeding of Your Toys, before you proceed so that you can make your selections armed with the knowledge of a smart consumer.

Vaginal Vibrations

For most women, the majority of nerve endings that respond to vibration are concentrated on the outside (vulva, clitoris) of the vagina, and in the first third of the vagina (also where the G-spot is found). The inner two-thirds tends to respond best to the feelings of fullness and rhythm. Keep this in mind when vibrator shopping: A penetrative vibrator with a vibrating tip won't matter much when the vibe's inside, but if the vibrating portion is seated at the base of the vibe, it'll be far more pleasurable.

The key to picking out the right first-time sex toy is making sure you select one with enough options to ensure that your lover can try a variety of ways to get off. When buying a vibrator, your first impulse might be to grab a Pocket Rocket or mini-massager because they're small, nonthreatening, and discreet—"they don't look like vibrators," you say to yourself. This might be a good choice if you know she's a little freaked out by the sometimes in-your-face way sex toys appear. But the drawback to a small one-speed vibe like this is that it has few options for the user—it's for clitoral stimulation only, so if she wanted to try vibration and penetration she'd have to get another vibrator, and because it has only one speed, that may not be *her* speed, if you get my drift. For first-time vibes, pick a basic model that's suitable for both clitoral stimulation and penetration, and that has variable speeds that can be changed as she feels the need to reach orgasm. Try a slimline or a dual-action vibrator, both excellent first-time choices.

As introduced in chapter 1, vibrators come in two very general styles: innies and outies. Some vibes are made for external

---

Butt Play Basics

- Insert a butt plug only when you're already really turned on.
- Never use a toy without a flared base.
- Don't insert items that can create a dangerous vacuum, like bottles.
- Use lots and lots of lube. Anal tissue is thin and doesn't lubricate itself, and can tear easily.
- If it hurts, that means you're going too fast, or you need more lube, or the item's too big, or you're not in the mood just now.
- Go slowly: very, very slowly.
- Read more in chapter 5, Strap-Ons and Bend Over Boyfriend.

---

stimulation (clit, nipple, penis head) while others are made for penetration—and some combine both. Vibrators can also be defined in two other distinct categories for use: multiple (variable) speed vibes, with vibrational intensity that can be adjusted as the user prefers, and vibrators with speeds that can't be changed—one-speed vibrators. Another duality in the vibrator world is the power source: batteries or electric power. Electric plug-in massagers are the most common (though rechargeable and even solar-powered models are on the market). Battery vibes are common, have no cord, and come in all styles, but never deliver a vibration as strong as one powered by juice from a wall outlet—which may or may not be important or useful to you. Further, vibrators can be innocuous and not look like a vibrator at all, or can be as fantastically realistic or cliché as you like. It all depends on what you want the vibrator to do, and how you want it to look, because even if you find the perfect size, shape, and controls, if it's ugly, it's just going to sit in a drawer making no one happy.

You should always choose first-time anal toys that follow the common-sense rules for anal penetration (see sidebar), meaning they should have a flared base so they won't get lost inside and should be made specifically for anal penetration. But the golden rule here is to always start small. That is, unless you know your lover likes size—and even then it's a good idea to err on the small side, because you can always upgrade later. Vibrating anal toys (like a small vibrating butt plug) are excellent first-time choices, as vibration will help relax the anal muscles and ease tension and discomfort. Also, be sure to get a toy with an absolutely smooth surface, as bumps or ridges might not go over well with an anal virgin (you can always experiment later with bumpy toys if it turns out they like butt toys).

Her first G-spot toy will need to be firm, slightly curved, and designed to supply G-spot stimulation. Not every woman likes G-spot play, so ask. Many women-run sex toy shops sell G-spot exploration kits specifically aimed at beginners; these are a great starter item. Typically, the main toy in these kits is a hard plastic or firm jelly rubber curved vibrator, as lots of women find that vibration makes G-spot exploration feel super good.

G-Spot Toys

The G-spot is an area of spongy erectile tissue generally 1 to 2 inches inside the vagina, on the front wall (belly button side), right around the urethra (where urine comes out). Some women like G-spot stimulation and others don't—simple as that. G-spot vibrators and dildos have a smooth, curved tip, and most G-spot aficionados say that the firmer the toy, the better. Hard plastic and firm silicone G-spot toys get high ratings.

Selecting the right dildo, like any other toy, will always be a matter of personal preference for size, shape, and appearance. But the function of the dildo is also key in determining what's right for the kind of play you have in mind. Do you want something smooth, ridged, slim, or with a bulbous head? If you're not sure what size or kind of dildo to get, take a minute to experiment with your fingers to get an idea about what size might appeal to you. Don't let your imagination and excitement lure you into buying a dildo that might be too big to start with, unless you know you really love the feeling of fullness. When looking at measurements online, know that width (or diameter) will mean the measurement across the dildo (as in a cross-section), not around it.

A guy's first cock ring should be as simple and easy to use as possible. As you learned in chapter 1, a cock ring is a ring worn around the penis and testicles to apply a steady pressure around the base, slightly restricting the blood flow to the penis to give a continuous squeeze to his penis and testicles. The simplest cock ring style is a single leather band with snaps, called a cock strap: It goes over the top of the penis's base and continues around and behind the testicles. Great beginner choices for cock rings also include very stretchy jelly rubber rings—these are usually colorful, made of soft jelly rubber, and sold in packs of four or more. They're great for experimenting with one, two, or more rings to increase or decrease constriction; because they're super-stretchy, cock rings made of jelly rubber can be taken off in a jiffy if they feel too tight.

Cock rings come in many types and styles—leather, fabric, neoprene, and various plastics and rubbers. Not all of them have snaps. Some fasten with Velcro, some tie or have sliding closures, and some are just rubber rings that stretch wide and slip on. A whole selection of complicated and torturous cock rings is available; you can find cock rings with multiple straps, ball stretchers, ball dividers, or D-ring attachments for weights, ties, or leashes. Again, your best advice is to start out with a single, simple ring, then see if your man likes it. You can diversify later.

Sex Toy Surprise: Ideas

- Before the present gets unwrapped, stun and delight your lover with an erotic treat, such as an aphrodisiac dinner or a full-body erotic massage, or read a sexy story together in your silk pajamas.
- Slip her a note telling her you have a naughty present for her later. Give it at precisely the right moment.
- Hint at what's to come that evening—give him a note with instructions to get ready for hot sex later, and leave an erotic picture that shows sex toys (like a sexy or vintage postcard) where he'll find it.
- Treat your lover to a session of really hot, aggressive sex, then give her the gift afterward, so she can think about the possibilities for the next round.
- Leave the present under his pillow to discover alone (or when you both slip under the covers).
- Tuck your gift into a bouquet of flowers.
- Hide the wrapped toy on your person and tell her to frisk you to find it.

The Fantasy Maker

In all your plotting to introduce erotic toys into your sex life, remember that the toy is merely a utensil to help you whip up a tasty sexual feast; it's not the meal itself. You'll want to think about what turns you both on, as you ponder your choice of toys. You both have a sexual fantasy, and you'll want to get the gift that'll make your fantasies come true. Excellent! Now just nail down the details of your sexual fantasy and you're ready to go shopping. Use the following guide to make the right toy selections.

Sex Act	Right Tools for the Job
Masturbation fantasies, her	Slimline vibe, dual-action vibrator, bullet vibe, wearable finger vibe (variable speed vibes a plus)
Masturbation fantasies, him	Cock ring, masturbation sleeve, vibrating penis cup, Fleshlight, lubricant
Anal play	Butt plug, vibrating anal wand, anal beads, dildo, and always lubricant
G-spot play, female ejaculation	Firm, smooth, curved dildo or vibrator and lubricant: can be glass, metal, hard plastic, or firm jelly rubber (variable speed vibes a plus)
Strap-on sex	Easy-on harness, lubricant, dildo
Threesome fantasy with two people	Dildo with suction cup base that attaches to wall, chair, or floor; sex machine; or harness that straps a dildo onto furniture or a pillow
Sexual power exchange	Restraints; sexual wearable such as nipple clamps, anal plug, or chastity belt; blindfold; ball gag; remote control vibrator; teledildonic device
Being sexually "used"	Sex machine; face or body harness with dildo; extreme restraints; sex sling or swing; sex furniture; collar and leash
Bondage	Ropes, cuffs, arm and leg bindings; blindfold; bondage travel kits (sold at specialty BDSM stores); feathers and soft fabrics—or spankers, riding crop, whips

Don't Forget the Lube!

If you've never tried lube, I insist that you buy a bottle immediately and see what you've been missing. Even if you think you
don't need it, try it anyway—this isn't about need, it's about
fun. Of course, if you're thinking of anal play, then you'll
absolutely require it, but the way lube makes slippery genitals
even *more* slippery is a sensation that has to be experienced to
really be appreciated.

Lube comes in a range of thicknesses, consistencies, flavors,
and styles. Finding the lube that's right for you will be a matter
of personal preference, though some people like different lubes
for certain activities, much like a cook will use a variety of sea-
sonings. You may prefer a lube that closely mimics natural vaginal
lubrication, like Liquid Silk. Or, for anal play, a thicker gel-like
lube such as Astrogel may do the trick. You might prefer long-
lasting silicone-based lubes like Eros Silicone for hand jobs.

Water-based lubes are the standard, as they clean up easily
with just water and are safe for the vaginal ecosystem to flush
out. Oils of any kind are difficult to flush from the vagina, so
skip the oily stuff—that goes for whipped cream and chocolate,
too. Some water-based lubes have sugars (also labeled glycerin,
glycerol, and natural flavor) that can be very irritating to some
women; since sugar feeds yeast, these can lead to yeast infections. Read the ingredients list before you use any lube, if you're
at all sensitive—colorings and flavors can have the same unde-
sirable effect. Water-based lubes (including silicone) are safe
to use with condoms and safer sex gear.

Lubricants with benzocaine and numbing agents such as
Anal Eze, "good head gel," and desensitizing creams contain oils,
flavors, and colorings, and are highly unsafe. Numbing the back

of the throat, the penis, the vagina, and especially the anus can lead to serious injury and infections that can (and often do) land users in the doctor's office or ER. Think about it: You can't feel the skin breaking or tearing, and if it's the anus, fecal bacteria are present too. When you can't feel pain, you're getting injured, period. Also unsafe are "shrink creams," which claim to make the vagina smaller or tighter. The key ingredient in these creams is alum (aluminum chloride, an aluminum compound). They absorb water from the outer layer of the skin; as more water is absorbed, the cells begin to swell, closing the ducts through which water would normally flow. No study has been done on the effect of these creams on the cervix, which is what they eventually end up getting rubbed on during penetration, but I'll wager it's not good.

Nevertheless, it's not all bad news. Flavored lubricants are a fun treat, and are readily available at any adult toy or novelty store. They generally don't taste very good; imagine the flavor of lube mixed with artificial flavoring and sweetener. Yum! The pictures on the labels look much better than the products taste—and you may want to ask yourself what you do (or don't) want to taste, anyway. Edibles come in two categories: lubricants that are water-based, and edible gels, liquids, or sprays that may contain oils. No matter how completely you think you are licking it off, even the smallest amount of oil can cause a condom, dental dam, or glove to break.

Not to say that licking something yummy off of your lover isn't fun—it is. It can be a treat to have a little something extra to lick, something that makes your strokes longer and more focused. The water-based brand ID Juicy Lube has by far the cleanest ingredient list, no artificial coloring, and the largest selection of flavors; I recommend sticking with its line of fruit flavors, though I admit Bubblegum Blast is a personal favorite. Hot Licks is a super-sugary-tasting line of water-based flavored gels that heat up when you breathe on them (though the heating-up sensation isn't for everyone), and they come in flavors like strawberry and cinnamon. Kama Sutra makes a whole range of products made for licking off excited body parts, and its Oil of Love product also heats up; but keep in mind that many products in this line contain trace amounts of oil.

Lube and Your Body

When it comes to making sex feel amazing, a high-quality lubricant is one of your best choices. Contrary to popular belief, using lube doesn't mean that someone isn't turned on. A lot of women find that their natural lubrication varies quite a bit, depending on where they are in their menstrual cycles. Starting or stopping hormonal birth control can affect vaginal lubrication, as can pregnancy, menopause, and anything else that affects hormone levels. For that matter, many common medications can affect lubrication. Did you know that antihistamines can dry out the vagina as well as your sinuses? Antidepressants, alcohol, marijuana, and even long-term cigarette smoking can all have the same effect. Unfortunately, many people still think that if a woman is turned on, she shouldn't need lube, so they assume there's something wrong. Plus, everyone needs lube for anal play, and lube increases the effectiveness of condoms.

There are lots of lubricants these days. Water-based formulas rinse away easily, but they tend to dry out. Glycerin is super slippery, but it gets sticky after a while. Non-glycerin lubes don't get sticky, but they don't last as long before soaking in, so you'll need to add more. Silicone lubricants never dry out, but they take soap and water to wash off skin, and they can damage some silicone toys, so cover your toys with condoms to avoid that.

Some newer lubricants are a blend of water-based ingredients and silicone. That makes them long-lasting and super slippery, but also easy to clean up. Look for "hybrid" lubes if that's what you're after. Thinner lubricants are often better for vaginal sex, while thicker gels are generally preferred for anal play since they give a little more cushioning.

If you've never used lube, give it a try. You might be surprised at how fantastic it makes sex feel!

—CG

Chapter 3

Come Together

You have no secrets from your sex toys. When in hand, your toys operate in tandem with your fantasies, bringing you to orgasm in a seamless session of self-love. Your sex toys never have a selfish moment during sex; nor do they come before you do, whether by accident or intention. They live to serve as your sex slaves, minus all the upkeep and the care and feeding of an actual sex slave (apart from batteries and soap). Machines never tire, and they never take it personally when you come quickly and just want to roll over and go right to sleep. Sex toys don't care what you fantasize about to get off, and they have no opinions on your choice of positions or porn. They also feel just fine if you change your mind midstroke, and decide to shut them off and put them away.

But being with another person is different. Your lover can't read your mind, nor can they vibrate—at least not as reliably as a Hitachi.

The big fantasy we all have is to orgasm with our lovers, at exactly the same time, in a big synchronistic moment of equally shared, pure bliss. Reality is often quite a bit different, especially during penetrative sex. For many, just having an orgasm at all during penetration is a challenge. There's a lot going on, and it's hard to focus. Sometimes it's a demanding process, not to mention the fact that when something feels really good, you probably feel that you look silly. But there's an easy answer, at least to the orgasm question: A playfully diverse world of toys and props exists to help us all meet our orgasmic goals, and to make sex into a delightful pleasure shared by two.

A good number of people think of sex toys only as solo tools for personal pleasure. Some even consider sex toy use by couples to be a signifier of things gone wrong, as if using a toy is akin to "cheating," or as if getting pleasure from something other than the way a couple "should" be having sex is bad or doesn't count. Or worse, that the couple are deviants or somehow perverted (in a bad way). But the truth is, a couple's exploration of their shared sexuality through use of sex toys is a healthy sign of a relationship that grows, stretches, and changes with time. It's a marker of a relationship with open communication, and it means that both parties are interested in deepening their intimacy and truly desire to make each other feel good. Because that's what sharing sex toys, and using them to come together, is all about. Play, desire, communication, and (of course) getting each other off—royally.

Incorporating toys into your shared sex life is easy if you first met at the vibrator store, or if you brought the subject up early in the development of your sexual relationship. Then, it's absolutely no problem for you to bring home a new butt plug tucked into a floral bouquet for your three-day holiday weekend at home. But if you've never really brought up the subject, or you formerly used toys but stopped awhile back and want to try them again, then it's going to seem a little risky to bring it up—but only at first.

Talk About It

It's really as easy, or as scary, as asking—because in bed as in life, if you want something, you're just going to have to ask for it. Once you get your courage up and ask, that doesn't always mean you'll be met with enthusiasm, or if you are, that your lover will be able to execute your desires in the ways you want. On the other hand, your request may just be the thing they've been hoping to hear, but have themselves been too afraid to ask.

Before you talk, think about how you might bring up the subject in a way that would feel safe for you. You might feel more comfortable watching a movie with a scene in it that's similar to your fantasy, then commenting on the scene. Or do you think you'd feel okay asking your partner what they think about sharing fantasies while you're entwined in an intimate cuddle? Another technique you can try is telling him you want to confess a fantasy—a sexual one—and that he isn't to reply right away. Tell him that you can have a conversation about it later; this gives both of you time to let the idea settle.

Consider ways in which you can encourage your partner to hear you out, and ask them to suspend judgment until you can explain why this is important, and how much fun you think the two of you will both have—and how important their participation is to you. Be sure to reassure him or her that you find them incredibly sexy, and that this wouldn't be happening unless you felt safe to tell them your deepest desires. Your lover needs to hear that they are the star of your show, in addition to the fact that you're ready to become closer than you've ever been before.

If you're the one bringing it up, reverse roles for a minute: If you don't normally talk about sex in your relationship and then suddenly one of you wants to, it might be upsetting—initially. Your lover may wonder if you've been holding back sexual secrets all along. But it's more likely that opening up to them about your sex toy fantasy will give them the opportunity to tell you what's on *their* mind about sex, too. Many couples discover that talking about sex is a pretty hot form of foreplay all on its own.

Ready, Set...Play!

When you're ready to experiment with your new toys, be sure that you have privacy and the elements necessary to make it as hot as it can get. Home and getaway weekends (in a hotel or bed-and-breakfast) are the best places to try out your toys, and with a little hot talk and imagination, you're free to play sexy mad scientist with each other's bodies to your heart's content.

Set aside time when you'll both be free of distractions, and can fully relax—turn off your phones, check that your roommates are really away, send the kids to a sitter. Make sure you've shopped for anything you might need, and don't forget the lube and batteries. Have these items prepared for your sexual adventure ahead of time, or, if you're visiting your lover's house, take your toys and treats with you. Most importantly, take a sense of sexual adventure and a sense of humor, because sex toy play is exactly that—*play*.

Sex toys don't always work the way they're supposed to, and it's crucial to remember this every time you turn on a funky vibrator, wrestle yourself into a strap-on, accidentally squirt lube onto your pillow, or try on a slippery cock ring. It's always going to be an experiment, and yes, someday you'll master the seductive art of slipping effortlessly into a harness and elegantly advancing on your excited prey. But the first several times, the buckles might be problematic, or the vibrator might be tricky to put batteries into, and it's difficult to look cool when you're squinting at the battery directions trying to figure out which way they go, while your lover gets cold—but remains hopeful for the moment the batteries snap in and you get down to business. That's why it's essential that both of you have a sense of humor about the foibles and failures of cheaply made and sometimes user-unfriendly sex toys. And always be prepared for the times when you both give up on making the damn toy work (or you unwrap it to discover it's shipped broken)...and just have hot sex anyway.

Expect the Unexpected (to Be Really Hot)
- Have your idea planned in advance; set the toys in an easy-to-reach area.
- Make sure you have everything you need or might want if things get super hot.
- Check all batteries and vibrators for function beforehand. Nothing's worse than battery failure at a crucial moment!

How to Introduce a Sex Toy in the Heat of the Moment
- Never blindside your lover without some kind of warning unless you know they're okay with sex toys.

- Smile and laugh, and really have fun—then, when you introduce the toy, you can carry the sexual merriment into your experiments.
- Start having sex the way you usually do, then ask if they mind if you try something a little different—something like the sex toy you have tucked in the nightstand drawer, ready to go.
- Tell your lover you heard about this great sex toy from a friend, so you bought one—and will your sweetie help you "test" it out? Like, right now?
- Tuck a toy under a pillow, and "discover" it at a particularly juicy moment in your lovemaking.
- Ask outright during sex, "Hey, wanna try this sex toy I just got?" Or, "Do you mind if I use a vibrator while you do that?"
- Buy a sex toy that's new to you both, and offer to put on a masturbation show for your lover with it. Upgrade: Have your lover hold the toy while you touch and bring yourself to orgasm. Double upgrade: Use the toy on yourself while you perform oral sex on your lover. Now *that's* a show.

Toys for Orgasm During Penetration

For many women, the primary key to orgasm during anal or vaginal penetration will be toys that provide adequate clitoral stimulation. Sure, your fingers are always ready to do the job, but often during penetration it's common to require firmer or more intense stimulation to take you over the edge. Also, intense clit stimulation can make anal sex much more pleasurable. Vibrators are the right tool for the job, and you have a number of options with which you can achieve your orgasmic goals.

Take those trusty fingers of yours, and modify them with a finger vibe. Choose from a wireless or cordless model and slip one on a fingertip—then let your fingers do the walking in all the right places. During penetration while on your back, you can easily reach your clit if your lover sits up. In a doggy-style position you can rest your torso on a pillow (or ottoman). In a woman-on-top position you can lean back and control his thrusts and your own clit stimulation easily—though note that this position might make your lover come faster than you'd planned, with

Illus. 5: Toys for Orgasm During Penetration

all the visual stimulation they get watching you use them as a sex toy. Also, you can give the finger vibe to your lover and let them massage your clit for a while too, and see where it leads.

The same techniques can be used with your trusty bullet (or egg) vibrator. Since most of these have battery packs and a cord (but have more control options and variable speeds, yay!), you can set the controls in an easily reachable spot at your side while you rub the bullet all over your clit in a variety of positions. Some retailers sell wearable bullet pouches that slide on like a pair of crotchless panties, keeping the vibrator in place while leaving you open for penetration, though the bullet will need to be readjusted often as it will likely move around during thrusting.

Many stores carry wearable vibrators that are all-in-one, panty-style units. These toys are designed for hands-free clitoral stimulation, though some are better suited for solo use than for penetration with a partner: most are worn like a G-string panty, making it difficult to use accurately during penetration. Others are crazy multistrap contraptions that you step into and wear like a crotchless panty over your hips, but can mean lots of orgasmic fun when they're in place. Most wearable vibes have a little animal shape (like a butterfly or hummingbird), are made of jelly rubber for the clitoral stimulator, and come with either a battery pack or a cordless remote. Some are waterproof, have multifunction controllers, and even have insertable portions for vagina or anus. The remote control models are one speed and tend to be rather loud, so if you're fantasizing about wearing the vibe out in public and handing the controller to your lucky lover, make sure it's somewhere loud, like a dance club or construction site.

But why should *she* do all the work, when *he's* got a perfectly good tool? My point exactly—make the penis (or dildo) doing the thrusting do double time by strapping on a vibrating cock ring. These ingenious devices work just like a regular cock ring (see chapter 1, Basic Models, and Care and Feeding of Your Toys), but also have a vibrator seated at the base for clitoral stimulation. Some cock rings have nonvibrating stimulators, meaning a silicone, rubber, or jelly bump of some kind that's intended to rub the clit during penetration. Reviews on these, however, are mixed as to whether they're effective (though they're great if vibrators aren't your cup of tea).

The cock ring provides a little bit of squeeze to keep him hard and firm (possibly a bit longer than usual), and the vibrator will also give him a little buzz. But these aren't exactly hands-free devices; sometimes the ring will slip around and you might need to reach down and set the vibrator on the part of your clit that feels best for you. Also, remember that unlike a finger or bullet vibe, you'll only be feeling the vibration right on your clit when he's all the way inside you. Doggy-style is the position least beneficial for vibrating cock rings, while woman-on-top is usually the best position for control, placement, and enjoyment.

Sex Toys and Oral Sex

Sex toys can make your oral sex session red-hot, and they can provide ways for the person going down to double their pleasure (and their fun). Meaning, you can use a toy on the person getting head to make them come like crazy, but you can make yourself come too by stimulating yourself as you lick and suck.

Also, sex toys can provide a nice momentary respite, so that you can continue stimulating your partner while you give your tongue, neck, or jaw a rest.

Cunnilingus

Many a woman (though not all) enjoys penetration during cunnilingus—that is, as long as you don't stop or interrupt her clitoral tongue bath. You'll already have your hands teasing and tantalizing her, and when she's turned on you can try inserting the dildo, your fingers, or the vibe just a little, then ask her what she wants you to do next. Would she like thrusting, stillness, to be licked and pumped simultaneously? Think about how sexy it would be to hear her say, "I want you to fuck me with that dildo while you lick me."

Keep in mind a few salient facts about how the vagina responds to penetration. In general, you'll want to thrust in and out, not up and down, side to side, or in a circle, unless you know she likes it. If you want to vary your thrusting with other creative movements, ask her specifically how she'd like you to move; some women prefer straightforward in-and-out movements to anything else, while others might like variations at different times of the arousal cycle.

The outer areas, such as the vulva and the opening of the vagina, contain more nerve endings than the vaginal canal and respond best to touch and vibration. The inner portion, inside the canal, has fewer nerve endings near the skin's surface and responds to feelings of fullness, pressure, and rhythm. A vibrator will therefore feel intensely good around the clitoris and the vaginal opening. Using a sex toy for penetration while you lick her clit may be more easily accomplished if you lick with your head at a slight angle, giving you ample room to thrust a toy with your hand. You can also hold the toy stationary while you lick, allowing her to control the stimulation with her hip movements. G-spot dildos and vibrators, combined with cunnilingus, can provide an earth-shattering experience for women who love G-spot play.

Honestly, you can use any kind of vibrator you want on her during cunnilingus, but some types will be easier to use than others. If she has a favorite, then by all means use it! Longer vibes typically employed for penetration (like a Slimline) can make her feel especially good, but finger vibrators and bullet vibes allow you to specifically buzz the spot where you last licked. When bringing a vibe into the action, start on the lowest speed, and give her more as she asks for it. Remember to never put the vibe directly on her clit right away; always start from the sides. Using a vibrator while you lick will vibrate your tongue and mouth and after a while may make you feel like your whole head is buzzing, but it can feel amazing to the recipient.

This is especially true for tongue vibes: small, cordless, watch-battery-powered vibrators that literally strap to your tongue and turn it into a vibrator that adds a buzz to whatever part of the anatomy you touch it to. The first question people ask about these vibes is, "Are they safe?" That seems to be a concern echoed by responsible retailers across the nation. While there is little to no chance of shock from an exposed mechanism in these toys, I can virtually guarantee that no one's done any kind of a clinical study on the effects of intense vibration in the mouth (or on TMJ, temporomandibular joint pain), or what happens should one of these toys get accidentally swallowed. While they're an awful lot of fun, they're not for long-term use, and to avoid mishaps they should be used soberly and carefully by the person with the toy in their mouth.

Fellatio

Cock rings add delightful constriction and tension to any blow job, and the resulting hardness from a well-applied ring makes the wearer's enjoyment readily apparent. This might be just the toy you need to make his orgasm one of the most intense he's ever had.

But some men really like vibrators, too. Choosing what to use on him during fellatio depends on what you have in mind. There are vibrators on the market for just about every scenario you can imagine, though in a pinch you can always use any type of vibe.

Men who like vibration have preferences as to how intense, where, and when in their pleasure cycle they like it. When you're not sure, ask him or have him show you. Generally speaking, vibration right on the head of his penis might feel too intense— popular spots where men like vibration are underneath the head, along the underside of the shaft (possibly at the base), and on his testicles (gently), perineum, or anus. Access to all these pleasure zones while you're going down on him is easiest when he's lying on his back. You can easily hold his penis in your mouth and vibrate the underside of the shaft, run the vibe over his balls, or push farther south if he's game. As with cunnilingus, you can use finger, bullet, and tongue vibes alternately as you suck and lick, or you can make them part of your licking, sucking, stroking finale.

Anal Toys

Butt plugs, anal beads, and vibrators and dildos that are safe for anal penetration can all be seamlessly incorporated into your usual lovemaking and oral sex styles to add pleasure and make orgasm more intense. Anal penetration is one of those amazing things that connect you with your lover like nothing else, and it can be an incredible turn-on for both of you. With a dildo, plug, beads, or a vibrator up one or both of your asses, you enter into a realm of pleasure that's as deep for your sweetie as it becomes intensely intimate for both of you. And in some people, it's like hitting a pleasure switch—even the lightest touch on the outside of the anus sends some people straight to orgasm.

Discussing anal play before you try it is a must, unless you and your lover already have sexual adventure on the menu. Anal play for someone who's not ready for it can be very unsettling; don't guess how he or she might react, because for some people anal penetration is going too far. So, how do you add butt toys to sex and make it pleasurable? Follow the three golden rules: Go very slowly, listen to the person you're penetrating or touching, and use lots of lube.

Read the "Butt Play Basics" sidebar in chapter 2, First-Time Toys and Gifts, before you even *think* about getting started. Much like the vagina, the outer third of the anus (and in men, the prostate) contains more nerve endings than the anal canal and responds best to touch and vibration. The inner portion, inside the canal, has fewer nerve endings near the skin's surface and responds to feelings of fullness, pressure, and rhythm.

Squirt liberal amounts of lube onto any toy you use, and reapply frequently. You can use a vibrator to lightly circle the anus, never going inside, which may be all the stimulation your lover needs to come. Or, insert a butt plug and keep it in place while you perform oral sex and bring your partner to orgasm at both ends; just don't leave it in for extended periods, or it will get uncomfortable. Chances are good that your lover's PC muscles will squeeze the plug out before they orgasm; if you like, you can hold the plug in place with your free hand. It can also get forced out during orgasm, which is an okay way to remove it. But if it's big and stays in place, after they come ask him or her to take a few deep breaths and let them know you're going to remove the plug on an exhale—then remove it on the second or third exhale.

Anal beads can give you thrills in a variety of ways, and experimentation leads the way to bliss. Some people like to insert the beads slowly, one at a time; others like to insert all of them and leave them in place while enjoying other sexual activities. The beads are usually pulled out before or at the moment of orgasm to heighten the sensation; they can be withdrawn deliciously slowly, or fast, like pulling an orgasmic rip cord.

Bullet and egg vibrators should only be used as external anal toys, and in no other way. Sure, some people claim that they can push these toys out of their ass at will, and it's common to see porn performers insert these toys into their anus and remove them with the cord or a quick squeeze of the sphincter muscles. But for every person practiced in the advanced yoga of sphincter control, there are dozens of people who have had embarrassing trips to the ER or made calls to crisis hotlines in desperation when one of these toys has gotten "lost" in the lower colon. I know; I've interviewed X-ray techs and ER orderlies and spoken with many crisis hotline operators who have fielded these calls. The toys are petite and smooth, so they're oh-so-tempting to insert for gentle internal anal vibrations. But the smaller and more cordless they are, the worse idea it is to put them inside. No one wants a vibrator that won't shut off buzzing, out of reach, inside their anus. Use bullets, small vibes, and finger vibes to lightly trace around the anal opening for a delicious tease and turn-on; then use a slim plug or dildo for penetration. You can always hold the vibe to the plug when it's in place to transfer the vibration to the deeper regions.

Chapter 4

Kinky Toys for Two

Kinky sex toys don't just drop into your life like ripe fruit. You have to procure them—*after* having a decadently kinka-licious fantasy that turns you on so much that you want to make it come true, in a fierce way. Nothing "makes" you kinky, and it's not in your DNA—it's *desire*. When you have fantasies about being paddled, or binding and gagging a lover, or giving fuzzy handcuffs as a gift (with the hopes of using them), or just doing something fetishy and taboo with a forbidden sex prop, then it's time to shop for toys. The toys described in this chapter prom-ise that one of you will give up erotic control and the other will take it—and this exciting, arousing exchange often involves cap-tivity or bondage, and may even involve punishment, erotic pain, or submission. Or, you may find both sides of the equation excit-ing, and in the compelling world of kinky toys, you can have your fantasies come true in any way you like.

You don't need to be a bondage whiz or a whip expert, speak S/M scenester lingo, or know a famous dominatrix to add a kinky toy to your arsenal and make a fantasy come true. All you need is an idea, a few safety tips, and some practical suggestions about shopping for the right gear. Many online retailers offer starter bondage kits, with quality that varies greatly. Avoid buying kinky toys from retailers who carry a lot of novelty toys (see chapter 1, Basic Models, and Care and Feeding of Your Toys, for a definition) to avoid ending up with cuffs that fall apart at your captive's first twitch. Instead, get your gear at places that specialize in kinky toys and have a good community reputation. They will have

Illus. 6: Toys for Bondage and Restraint

selected even their least expensive kits with care, and there you can find a basic setup with wrist and ankle bonds, a blindfold, and usually a little whip or a feather—all at an entry-level price.

Bondage, Handcuffs, and Sexy Restraints

Hundreds of erotic shopping options are available for buying bondage gear, from inexpensive steel handcuffs and nylon restraint kits, to ultradecadent leather-and-fur-lined locking cuffs, to exquisite lace-up arm binding (and body-binding) contraptions that look like haute couture. Deciding what you want is a matter of assessing what you might want to do, what you can afford, and how you visualize yourself (and your lover) in bondage—because bondage is just as much a visual turn-on as it is physically arousing.

After you decide what you both want, make sure everyone's on the same page and ensure that you'll both stay there by getting clear agreement that both of you want to do all these wonderful, wicked, deviously dirty things to each other. Make sure that everything regarding your mutual decisions to tie, bind, spank, whip, suck, and fuck is all crystal-clear, and don't deviate from those decisions unless they beg really, really nicely. Establish a "safeword" just in case things get a little too intense; decide on an unusual word that means "stop," "slow down," or "more, more!" Many people use stoplight colors, freeing up the more-instinctive words "stop" and "no" for moments of playful erotic protest.

Erotic bondage requires some kind of binding agent: ropes, metal handcuffs, leather cuffs, chains, or other items suitable for restraint. Silk scarves, neckties, and pantyhose look great in the movies, but in reality make poor (and not very safe or effective) tie-downs. In general, anything that stretches or can create ultratight knots can cut off circulation or be difficult to undo—an arousal killer, for sure. Beginners will want to dip their toes into the bondage pool with something that's inexpensive and easy to use, and that offers plenty of options. Wrist bondage is where it all begins: handcuffs, nylon or leather cuffs, or rope. Never lay anyone on top of their own bound or handcuffed wrists; it's unpleasant and you can unwittingly do nerve damage. From wrist restraints, you can progress to ankles, and perhaps waist, thighs, and chest bondage (never bind anyone by the neck, *ever*, and never leave anyone in bondage alone, for safety's sake). You can while away your time, erotically teasing, tormenting, and satisfying your lover as they're tied to the bed, to themselves, or to a chair, cuffed, restrained spread-eagled, or anything else you can cook up. Add standard sex toys like vibrators and dildos to bondage for a *real* thrill ride. Role-play scenarios will offer lots of creative possibilities, such as medical fantasies involving bandages and medical-themed sex toys like butt plugs used as thermometers or vibrators used for "nerve response" testing. Jail fantasies might feature imaginary bars and cages, but real metal handcuffs. Animal scenes with collars, harnesses, and leashes will also involve erotic grooming with finger vibes, plus really kinky harnesses with insertable dildos.

Rope bondage is sexy and alluring and can look like a gorgeous work of art when completed. Also, with rope you can create some of the more functional, custom-made body harnesses around; this is when someone's bound in a constricting torso harness similar to a dog harness, giving the person in charge the ability to move the submissive around by rope "handles," bind genitals into the harness for intense sensations when the submissive moves about, or control the sub's movements by fastening their harness to something (like a leash or tie-downs).

Learn about tying and untying a few basic knots before you even get a rope near someone's body, and experiment in increments. Visit the website http://en.wikipedia.org/wiki/knot for a complete list of knots, as well as links to resources that tell how to tie them, including sites with video instructions in several formats. A great hands-on instruction book on basic knots is the *Klutz Book of Knots*, which comes with rope and firm cutout pages with instructions for learning all the basics. Knots you'll want to learn about are the square knot, hitch, loop knot, lark's head, cinch loop, and something called a "gi" knot.

Buy soft nylon rope, not cotton, which will stretch and you'll end up tying your knots too tight without knowing it—some rope bondage kits include some of the most dangerous rope to play with, proving that many novelty retailers don't have a clue about BDSM or safety. Get your rope from kinky sex toy retailers who know their stuff, or at the hardware store: a good start-up kit is four lengths of soft nylon rope, each 4 feet long, with masking tape wrapped around the ends to prevent fraying.

Confinement, servitude, and subjection all fall into captivity scenarios. Bondage, submission, and being on the receiving end

Tie Me Up?

Before anyone gets tied up, it's absolutely required that you carefully discuss what will happen. It must be perfectly clear that you both want to try it, and the receiving partner must give explicit consent. Save the surprises for strip-o-grams and boxes of chocolates—not bondage.

of whatever the dominant dishes out are all the order of the day. With luck, your scenario involves some type of sex, and you may decide whether or not your scene involves pretend, previously agreed-on force or coercion. The person in charge might be doing it "for their own good," as therapy—or might be forceful, "making" the submissive comply sexually—or might pretend to trade sexual favors for their silence.

Keep medical scissors handy in case your knots are too tight, your bondage is painful or cuts off circulation, or your lover needs to get out of whatever it is, fast. Tie a long colorful ribbon to your handcuff key so it's impossible to lose. And remember— if you restrain them in public, you'll probably wind up in jail.

Okay, so that all sounds hot. But you must be wondering, "Once I get my lover tied up, what the hell do I do then?" Good question, and I have a few ideas for you.

- Blindfolds are a great way to keep them guessing what's next.
- Strip, or masturbate, just out of reach.
- Tell them how helpless and vulnerable they are. And all the things you might—and *will*—do to them.
- Rub their body slowly with fur, feathers, silk, satin, scratchy wool, panties, whips, or any fetish objects.
- Give them an erotic massage.
- Bite and scratch, spank and slap (not the face or testicles).
- Have your way with them sexually—very slowly, or rough and quick.
- Try hot and cold sensations from ice, warm tea bags, or changing the temperature of your mouth. Never put ice inside anyone.
- Drip hot wax on them.

- Alternate pleasurable pain with masturbation.
- Apply clamps and clips to their body—buy these in a specialty fetish store, and don't leave them on for more than 5 minutes.
- If tickling arouses your lover, have at it.
- Oral sex—giving or receiving. Face-sitting is nice, too.
- Shave their genitals.
- Use sex toys on them.
- Something missing? How about seeing how they look wearing a butt plug that has a fuzzy bunny tail, feather, or horsie tail coming out the end!

Blindfolds and Gags

One toy I feel that everyone should have in their toybox, no matter if they're kinky or not, is a blindfold. When wearing a blindfold, you can completely surrender to your lover's erotic whims, you never know what's coming next, the suspense arouses you incredibly, and you have a wonderful feeling of risk, trust, and delicious erotic expectation—all at once. Putting a blindfold on someone is a thrill beyond compare; here you have a love slave whom you can surprise, tease, turn on, and make come without their even needing to know what's next on the menu. Plus, if you're nervous or confused, or have to struggle with a stubborn vibrator battery case, they'll never know, because they'll just be sitting there in suspense for the next trick you have up your sleeve. And it totally doesn't matter what your hair looks like when your lover can't see you.

Satin blindfolds are usually the least expensive and most widely available, though they have a tendency to slip around and leave

corners of sight exposed—making them fine for your first experimentation, but not the best choice. Good nylon models are a
solid choice, and should have one nice, thick elastic strap across
the back (not two) and a padded or faux-fur-lined interior.
Blindfolds at the kinky sex shop come in hundreds of colors,
materials, and designs, from white leather with red crosses for
nurse and medical scenes to fake-leopard fur and beyond. Leather,
rubber, and custom blindfolds lie in the more expensive range,
but they're worth it, as they tend to be made with exceptional
quality and for your comfort; hourglass-shaped blindfolds provide the best coverage. Be sure that your blindfold isn't too tight,
that any fake fur isn't going to get in your lover's eyes, and that
if your partner wears contact lenses they might want to remove
their lenses, use a looser blindfold, or only wear the blindfold
for a limited time. And if you travel overseas to visit your lover
and forget your blindfold, don't panic—a blindfold (cleverly
called a "sleep mask" by airline attendants) will be provided for
your in-flight comfort, and your postflight enjoyment.

The same sorts of rules apply for gags. A gag fills the mouth
and either ties at the back or is held in place with a single elastic or leather strap, sometimes adjustable. A ball gag is the classic
style: It's simply a strap with a ball made of rubber, plastic, or
leather that fits in the mouth and adds a layer of helplessness
to your submissive lover's predicament. Ball gags will have
different sized balls, so know that some balls will be too big
for a comfortable fit, and if your lover has jaw issues or TMJ,
then perhaps a nonball style will be a better substitute. If you
gag your sweetie, establish a physical safeword (like releasing
or dropping an object like a ball or a bell), and watch for jaw
cramp or too much of the gag in the mouth, which might cause

a gag reflex. Be very careful not to bump or accidentally hit the face or jaw when the gag is in place, thus avoiding injury. Some gags have really kinky extras inside for the submissive to suck on, such as pacifiers or mock cocks. Yum.

Sex with Paddles, Whips, Clamps, and Clips

Ever fantasized about getting swatted with a paddle, or even a whip, during sex? You're not alone, and you've got a mind-

Illus. 7. Paddles and Whips

Good Pain

Be absolutely clear about what's "good" pain and what constitutes "bad" pain. Find out what your lover likes about it; ask specific questions, and make sure to agree on specific things that they want you to do. This is called *negotiation*—you're agreeing on desires, activities, and, most important, limits. Decide on a *safeword*—a word that your lover will say when they absolutely want you to stop. Don't ask if something is "okay," because that word can mean anything. Ask whether they want it harder, softer, or tighter, more pinch or less movement, or whether you should stop.

boggling array of options for making your fantasies come true. The threshold of mingling pleasure with pain can be crossed in a variety of ways. The two of you may have decided that you want to add kinky pain to your usual sex play, and so you simply experiment with techniques and toys. Or, you could have a fantasy scenario in mind in which one of you is dominant while the other is submissive, and a kinky pain-toy fuels your fantasy's fire.

Whatever the case, it's essential to remember that we're using kinky toys to *enhance* sex, not strangle it, so always remember to sexually stimulate your lover when you're doing wonderfully wicked things to them with kinky sex toys. Use the endorphins and adrenaline from the pain to enhance the chemical cocktail of their sexual pleasure; alternate pain with oral sex, hand jobs, and even when you lustily penetrate your lover into orgasmic bliss. When administering pain and blending it with pleasure, be sure to give your lover *almost* what they want, then back off and make them want it, bad. Don't go for the intense sensations right away; go lightly at first, then give a little more.

You can administer and vary the levels of pain in myriad ways. Types of stimulation that kinky toys can provide include friction, pressure, fullness, pinching, slapping, constriction, spanking, flogging, heat or cold, caning, and more—and you can use these in a plethora of styles. You might spank or slap with a toy like a paddle made of leather, wood, metal, or rubber, and you might alternate oral sex or manual stimulation (a hand job) with your spanks. A flogger is a multitailed whip that can

Illus. 8: Clamps, Clips, and Pinwheel

deliver sensations from dull and "thuddy" to sharp. You can lightly whip genitals with a small flogger, as that size of flogger is good on sensitive areas; you can use larger (medium-sized) floggers for backs, butts, and thighs.

Riding crops and canes hurt quite a bit because they quickly impact a small, concentrated area of skin, though lightly tapping them on genitals and nipples can be a menacing turn-on. Canes, crops, long floggers, and long paddles provide a nice reach so that you can smack your lover's behind as they perform oral sex on you.

Pain enthusiasts enjoy clamps and clips, which deliver concentrated pinching sensations to the body part they're applied to. They pinch at first, then turn into a steady buzz of pain; then, when you take them off, sensation (blood) rushes to the area and there's a burst of intense pain. Get to know the pain cycle of clips by trying one on yourself, in a sensitive area like the inside of your arm, and you'll see that while they hurt going on, they hurt much more coming off. Limit the time you keep the clip on; you should take them off after 15 to 20 minutes to avoid tissue damage.

Nipple clamps usually have a chain between them that can be pulled, tugged, or just allowed to hang and let gravity do the pulling as you move about during sex. Vibrating nipple clips can be used anywhere, and feel wonderfully intense (though heavy ones tend to fall off—look for petite models).

Clips and clamps can be strummed, tapped, or twisted (oww!) with your fingers. When the clips are on and you're performing oral sex, you can give your lover bursts of pain (reminding them that the clips are there) by simply touching them, pulling on the surrounding skin, or flicking the clamps with your fingers.

Pulling and twisting hurts even more. If you put clips on the penis, testicles, or outer labia, you don't have to avoid them during oral sex; indulge yourself and lick and suck on the clips, or lick and suck everything, clips and all. You can wrap rubber bands around larger clips to make them tighter or to pull several together. Lay a piece of thin cotton or nylon rope under a row of clips, and pull on one end of the rope as you would on a zipper, removing the clips slowly or in one blindingly painful zip—while fucking your partner. You can also rig ropes and clips to small fishing weights (available where fishing supplies are sold) for a steady pull with gravity's aid.

Apply clips to any area where you can pinch enough skin for the clamp—but use common sense and don't try to put a clamp on a flat area or an area where it's difficult to get some skin between your fingers. Smaller nipples are harder to clamp, and you'll need to experiment with different styles to see what works; the same goes for large nipples, but there's a variety of clamps made specifically for big nipples, such as tweezer clamps.

Little clamps can be purchased practically anywhere, from a fetish boutique to a stationery store. Clamps and clips made specifically for S/M play are best for sex. These have already been designed for sexual purposes, taking into consideration that they might be going onto sensitive areas or thin skin. Small clips are usually plastic with a spring that you pinch open, though you can also find metal versions. Even though a clip may be small, it can be pretty mean, because it concentrates the pain in one small area. Medium to large clips can be plastic or metal, even similar to the clips you'd use to keep a bag of potato chips fresh. Make sure that the ends of any metal clamps are padded or encased in rubber, and that any clips you use have no teeth.

Wooden, plastic, and specialty metal clothespins fall into the "mean" category. Clothespins are intense. Be sure to always test each clothespin before you use it, as they have differing intensities, depending on how tight the spring is. You can lessen the pinch by forcing the spring open slightly with a pair of pliers. Nipple clamps often have a way to adjust the pressure, such as a slide ring on tweezers, or a tightening screw on alligator clamps. These are fun because you can vary the pressure on whatever body part you've clamped—for instance, you can increase pressure by tiny increments as arousal increases.

Hot Wax

When dripped slowly and sensuously, hot wax can be the perfect combination of pain, suspense, peril, and pleasure for the receiver—plus, it's lots of fun to be the one holding the candle and orchestrating the suspense. Use common sense when playing with candles; keep the flame away from skin and bedding, don't set the candle near an open window or curtains, extinguish all flames before switching activities, and so on.

Most kinky retailers will sell candles made especially for hot wax play. When selecting candles, use plain white, unscented varieties. Never use beeswax, which can cause serious burns. The burning sensation from wax play should last for a minute, then fade, and not leave actual burn marks that linger for more than a few minutes. The closer you hold the candle as you drip the wax, the hotter the burn; the higher up you hold the candle, the less hot the wax when it lands on the skin. Some companies make "massage candles" made of a scented soy wax that stays liquid once it's melted, so you can drip mildly hot wax on your lover, then give them a massage with the warm oil. These are wonderful toys for erotic massage play, though the oils will ruin safer sex gear. It should be noted that massage candles might make for the most intense hand jobs your guy's ever had.

More Ouchy Fun

You can also play with a prickly pinwheel (called a Wartenburg neuro wheel, for those in the know), a device doctors use on your body to determine nerve response. At home, you can use it everywhere except on the genitals, directly on the nipples, or on the anal opening. This sinister-looking and very painful medical instrument consists of an 8-inch handle, with a small stainless steel rolling wheel at one end that has sharp pinpricks. When the wheel is rolled lightly over skin, like a pizza wheel, it leaves a trail of sharp pain and a fiery sensation in its wake. Make sure you roll it lightly to avoid piercing the skin. And don't share your pinwheel with other partners, unless you have access to hospital sterilization.

Cock rings shouldn't hurt when they're on, but they can be made to, and you can find ones that are made for pain rather than constriction. Rings can be tightened, or layered one on top of the other to up the ante. Some cock rings have steel D-rings on them, allowing you to attach a fishing weight or a leash; fishing weights should be gently lowered with your hand, and leashes should never be yanked on. Ball stretchers, cock and ball vises, ball stocks, ball separators, and combination cock ring/ball "torture" (CBT, or cock-and ball torture) devices can all be found at specialty S/M boutiques, especially ones that cater to gay men. These toys will bring out the Inquisitor in you, and ideally will evoke delighted moans of pleasurable pain from him, but only experienced players should use them.

If intense sensations like clamps, spanking, whipping, paddling, and other types of pain sound like the ingredients for a hot date, follow these guidelines and suggestions:

- Start slowly, and always increase sensation slowly.
- Begin with light sensation. Use the toy to caress, knead, lightly slap, and spank.
- Speak in role, whisper dirty talk, or say things to excite your lover the entire time. Make it part of your dialogue to ask how they like it; this is also how you can tease out what they want next.
- Alternate different sensations—such as fur, satin, heat, ice, hot wax, biting and scratching—with your spanking or whipping.
- Never strike the lower back, head, neck or face, or bony areas such as the spine or knees.
- Give your lover a hand job as you go along.
- In a 69 position, you can spank or penetrate him or her while they perform oral sex on you.

Chapter 5

Strap-Ons and Bend Over Boyfriend

Have you ever wanted to turn the tables on your lover, strapping on a sexy black harness, fastening in a dildo to jut out from between your legs, just so—then following through with everything your new dick implies? And what would that entail, exactly: strutting around in a pair of high heels, or going all the way and dressing extra butch in a tank top and work boots? Better yet, if you followed all these lines of thinking, how hot and bothered would you get while stroking your new erect appendage, rubbing it all over your lover's face, and having them give you a blow job—or more, when you take total control and penetrate them?

Sound hot? It is. Being on the receiving end (literally) of a strap-on is just as arousing in the, well, flesh. Whether it's a power exchange fantasy, a gender-bending scenario, or just the blissful sensation of feeling your lover inside you, there's little that compares with strap-on sex.

Harnesses come in a variety of shapes, styles, and sizes, and can be tailored to fit virtually any fantasy scenario you and your lover have in mind. Strap-ons are for women, men, and trans people of all genders and orientations who want a little (or a big) something extra in their pants. There are strap-ons made just for men, harnesses for female-to-male trans folks, strap-on rigs made for a variety of functions like double penetration, and much, much more. Unlike their depictions in most porn, strap-ons aren't just for long-fingernailed, fluffy-haired, fake lesbians.

As a sex act, straight couples playing with strap-ons has proven a very lucrative, popular, emerging (and exciting) area of sexual expression. For those toy companies savvy enough to understand what's at play here, that is—because the "bend over boyfriend" phenomenon has befuddled the more traditional sex toy retailers and porn directors, and also sex advice authors and porn reviewers of all orientations. As noted sexologist Dr. Carol Queen said in the introduction to the how-to instructional video that coined the sex act's namesake (*Bend Over Boyfriend*), "Straight couples are reinventing anal sex." Because even if uptight porn directors and novelty manufacturers may not have the faintest idea why a couple buys a harness, it's certain that they're doing it because it's *fun*.

Wearing a strap-on, even if you don't do anything with it, is an encounter full of revelations and gives you a sense of sexual giddiness that must be felt to be understood—in addition to the incredible arousal that usually comes with playing with "your dick." Strap-on play has no unwanted consequences, like pregnancy or an STD. Being penetrated and played with by a lover in a harness is just as fun, intense, and sexually exciting as doing the strapping, and the orgasmic potential is eye opening. Although this chapter is written primarily for heterosexual couples, anyone looking to play with harnesses will want to give it a skim, as it's full of crafty ideas for shopping for, playing with, and coming with the aid of a strap-on harness.

Strap-Ons for Straight Couples

Straight couples *have* reinvented anal sex, and the *Bend Over Boyfriend* phenomenon brought on by the how-to video of the same name has skyrocketed harness and dildo sales to hetero-sexual couples across the nation. Perhaps the fact that straight men are interested in receiving anal exploration from their female partners comes from increased awareness about prostate pleas-ure—sometimes called "the male G-spot." Or maybe men are just more comfortable with and confident about their sexual-ity and can see through all the contrived myths linking male anal sex and homosexuality. And maybe now they feel free to make up their own minds about what they like, because in fact not all gay men like anal sex, and because being penetrated can't *make* someone gay. But most likely, because our culture talks about sex more than ever before, happy, horny, and adventur-ous guys and gals are looking at each other's bodies like the pleasure playgrounds they were meant to be. And that's a *really* good thing.

Penetration is one of those amazing things that connect you with your lover like nothing else, and it can be an incredible turn-on for both of you. When you plug a man with your finger or fingers, a dildo, or a vibrator, you enter into a realm of pleas-ure that's as deep for him as it is intimate for both of you. And for some men it's like hitting a pleasure switch—even the light-est touch on the outside of the anus shoots him straight to orgasm.

In almost every sex book you pick up, if you can find a reference to the prostate gland at all (without its being exclusively related to cancer), you'll notice a few strange things about the way authors deal with the subject. Many impart a homophobic tone that makes even *me* wonder if I'm repressing anything—and this goes for both male and female authors. It's as if they wanted you to be absolutely sure they're straight when they're telling you about what's inside guys' butts, and that you are too, and that everyone's still straight after they read about it. The concept of male anal penetration obviously carries a lot of stigma and shame for these authors. This would be funny if it weren't so frustrating trying to get practical sex information out of their books. The other unfortunate thing most books do when they cover real-life, try-this-at-home prostate stimulation (which they do rarely) is rush through the material and present it in a cold context, as if no one would really try this for pleasure. Oh, and did I mention that prostate play, or the enjoyment thereof, has nothing to do with sexual orientation? It doesn't. End of discussion.

The prostate gland is located at about the center of the male urogenital system, inside the perineal wall. It sits just below the bladder, producing the fluid that mixes with semen in ejaculate, and is connected to the urethra, the muscles that line the perineum, and the sphincter muscle. If there's an epicenter to male orgasm, then this must be it. Many men, though not all, find that when they're aroused, prostate stimulation is intensely pleasurable; that's because the nerve pathway from the brain to the penis runs through the rectum, and one large nerve bundle is located just beneath the prostate. Additionally, the root of the penis is more or less anchored at the prostate, so when you massage a guy's prostate you also transmit sensation to the base of his penis. If he experiences any pain when his prostate is touched, he should have it checked by his doctor. Men often describe the orgasms they have from prostate stimulation as deep, intense, and powerful.

His First Alien Probe

Many men (though not all) enjoy penetration during other sexual activities, like fellatio, hand jobs, or intercourse—that is, as long as you don't stop or interrupt direct stimulation of the penis. If you've talked to him about penetration beforehand, you've got it under control and are way ahead of the game. Discussing anal play before you try it is essential, unless you and your lover already have anal adventure on the menu. Starting anal play with someone who's not ready for it can be very unsettling; don't guess how he might react, because for some guys anal penetration is going too far. So, how do you add anal penetration to your sexual repertoire and make it pleasurable? Again, follow the three golden rules: Go very slowly, listen to the man you're penetrating, and use lots of lube.

Fingers are perfect for first-time penetration, as they afford you the most sensitivity and control. When he's turned on and ready to be fingered, you can start the experiment by massaging his buttocks and caressing the crack between his cheeks. If he responds positively, try slowly sliding a wet finger over the opening to his anus while you're kissing him, or while playing with his penis or testicles. Be sure your hands are clean (read: *scrubbed*—no dirt or grime under your nails) and your fingernails are trimmed and filed smooth. Make sure you don't have any tiny cuts or hangnails. Latex gloves or nitrile (nonlatex) gloves are excellent to use, because they provide a perfectly smooth, clean surface and you can simply take them off when you switch activities.

With the flat of your finger, or fingers, press lightly on the opening and hold it there. Increase the pressure a little, massaging and pressing in circular motions. Go very slowly, and listen to his cues or verbal instructions—for some guys, just having their anus touched is all it takes to push them over the top. Pay attention to sufficient lubrication, and never rely on saliva. In porn films they make it look like that's all they use, but that's not the case—they just don't show you the anal suppositories and numerous applications of lube. Experienced players can buy lube injection rigs from kink-friendly sites like stockroom.com.

If you know he's ready for insertion, if you're keeping him nice and hard, and if he's at the point when he's not sure whether he should be thrusting into your mouth or bucking onto your hand, check your accessories. You should have plenty of lube, plus gloves or finger cots. The anus is an unlubricated area; it does not self-lubricate like a mouth or vagina, and its skin is thin enough to abrade easily. Use lube, lots of it. You can never have too much lubricant. Use a thick, water-based lube. Have your gloves ready, or already on.

Move your flattened fingers in a circular motion, and begin experimenting with penetration by pressing one well-lubed finger at the base of the opening (toward his perineum). Massage the opening's base, and ask him if he wants you to go farther. Slowly slide your finger in up to the first joint (about an inch), or use a slim sex toy like a small butt plug, and hold it there for a few breaths. You'll feel the ring of muscles around his opening squeeze and contract—just stay still as the muscles relax.

When you feel the muscles relax, slowly slide your finger in a little bit more, then back out, doing a gentle in-and-out, not all the way in yet. Once again, this may be all it takes for him to come, or to decide that it's not what he wants right now—but if he does want more, follow his directions and body language from here on as you progress to more stimulation. You can go deeper or faster, or even add more fingers—but the rule of thumb (so to speak) is to do everything so slowly that you can practically feel the seasons changing around you. Anal penetration hurts when you go too fast, or you don't use enough lube, or the recipient isn't relaxed, or he really doesn't want to be doing it.

Once he's anally warmed up and ready for more penetration, you can bring sex toys into play. Vibrators will feel fantastic on his ass, and you can tease and penetrate him while you suck, stroke, or fuck him. The thing to know about vibrators and anal stimulation is that the outer third of the anus, and the prostate, contain more nerve endings than the anal canal and respond best to touch and vibration. The inner portion, inside the canal, has fewer nerve endings near the skin's surface and responds to feelings of fullness, pressure, and rhythm.

So, a vibrator will feel intense (intensely good) around the opening and pressing on the prostate. But the vibration won't be a factor deep inside—rather, the size, shape, and motion of the vibrator itself will. To maximize your buzz, select insertable vibrators that have the vibration located at the base. When bringing a vibe into the action, start on the lowest speed, and give him more as he asks for it.

Squirt liberal amounts of lube on any toy you use, and reapply frequently. You can fuck the daylights out of him anally with a dildo he likes. Or, insert a butt plug and keep it in place while you bring him to orgasm; just don't leave it in for extended periods, or it will get uncomfortable. Chances are good that his PC muscles will squeeze the plug out before he orgasms; if you like, you can hold it in place with your free hand. It can also get forced out during orgasm, which is an okay way to remove it. But if it's big and stays in place, after he comes ask him to take a few deep breaths and let him know you're going to remove the plug on an exhale—then remove it on the second or third exhale.

Strap-Ons and Dildos

When choosing a strap-on, take into account what kind of strap-on fantasy scenario you have in mind—pretty much any fantasy can be realized if you know the limitations of the market and how to get around them.

Newcomers to strap-on play will want to make their first purchase an inexpensive harness made of fabric or nylon with an inexpensive rubber dildo in a pleasing and reasonable shape. Options for harnesses range from neoprene and nylon to glittery vinyl, rubber, see-through plastic, leather, and velvet. Many online retailers have beginners' strap-on kits, though I suggest that you purchase these from reputable (nonnovelty) retailers so that you get quality products that will actually do what they're supposed to do, even if the kit is inexpensive.

All too often, novelty toy retailers mass-produce badly made harnesses out of fabric and elastic straps, which tend to fit terribly, have the dildo rest in the wrong place, and are often so loose that the dildo winds up doing embarrassing things when you're trying to repeatedly thrust and pull out. A good harness will have a secure method of attachment, as in wide straps made of elastic, leather, or nylon, plus buckles or D-rings that let you tighten the harness to your body.

Harnesses come in two general styles: a single-strap model that's worn like a G-string panty with the strap down the ass crack, and a two-strap model, with straps that run from the pubic bone, along the crease between the inner thigh and genitals,

Illus. 9. Harnesses

How a Strap-On Should Fit

The straps should be tight enough to withstand thrusting, but not so tight they pinch or cut into your skin; put the dildo in place and give it a few tugs to see how it feels. The dildo shouldn't slip out or slip around too much (though a little movement is fine). The dildo should rest right on or just above the wearer's pubic bone; if you get sore from thrusting, you can buy a specially made pad of thin foam to cushion your pubic bone.

---

underneath the buttocks, and attach to the waistband in back, like a jock-strap. Some prefer the G-string style, saying that it provides a stable base for the dildo and rubs the clit nicely when thrusting; others complain of "buttcrack rash" from the center string rubbing on their anus and tailbone. Another complaint about the G-string style is that it limits access to the wearer's genitals, so if a girl wanted to be penetrated or rub her clit while wearing the harness, it would be difficult. Also, this type isn't adaptable for male wearers.

Two-strap harnesses allow for plenty of genital access so that the wearer (of any gender) can masturbate or penetrate themselves, or be penetrated by a partner, while wearing the harness. For instance, a girl wearing a two-strap can jack off her cock with one hand or get a blow job, while she rubs her clit and fucks herself with a dildo at the same time—increasing her chances of fulfilling the fantasy of coming "with her big cock."

You'll also face choices when selecting a harness when you decide how you want the dildo attached to or worn in the harness. Some strap-ons will have a simple hole in the middle, where the dildo is pulled through from the inside; while these are the easiest to get dildos into and out of, it's a "one size fits most" hole that will have smaller dildos sliding around and bigger dildos difficult (or impossible) to squeeze in. A harness with a hole is especially suited for the unique line of double dildos made by Vixen, which penetrate both partners at once with the thrusting of the harness. Versatile harnesses have four straps that come through a triangle-shaped base and attach to a removable rubber O-ring in the center. This style provides far and above the most stable base for a dildo. O-rings can be purchased in several sizes (many of these harnesses ship with three ring sizes), and clean-up is a breeze.

The material you choose for your strap-on is up to you. I prefer leather for warmth and appearance, and buckles for no-slip fastening, but for airports or travel you might want to acquire a second model of fabric or neoprene; both types are machine washable, making them nice for clean-up. Leather should always be cleaned according to leather care instructions (search online or follow the manufacturer's care instructions), while rubber, plastic, and PVC strap-ons can be cleaned with an antibacterial wipe-down.

Selecting the best dildo for male anal penetration will, of course, be up to him, but I recommend getting a dildo that's

Do Men Wear Strap-Ons?

You bet men wear strap-ons, and do amazing things with them. There's no shame in the fun you can have with a man who can fuck you with two penises at the same time (anally and vaginally). Hello, double penetration fantasies! Or how about a man who knows he can make you come *again*, even after he already has? Double yum.

How to Come in Your Harness

- Masturbate yourself.
- Slip on a finger vibe and rub your clit.
- Slide a bullet vibe into the harness.
- Look for a "coupler" sleeve at sex shops that attaches to the harness to hold a dildo inside you.
- Slip into a wearable vibrator before you don your harness. Take turns with the controls.

not contoured, bumpy, or wider at the base than the top. Pick a smooth, slender dildo for his first strap-on adventures. The sphincter muscles are a ring about 1 to 2 inches deep, and wide-based dildos put uncomfortable stress on the guy's (possibly already tense and worried) muscles by stretching them on the "in" thrust. A bulb at the end is fine, and can be helpful for prostate stimulation, but remember you'll then be putting the biggest part in first, which might be too intense for your virgin. Read more about selecting a dildo in chapter 1, Basic Models, and Care and Feeding of Your Toys.

Fun Things to Do with Your New Dick

- Have him show you how he likes to jack off—but with your dildo.
- Get a sloppy blow job.
- Rub it all over his face.
- Lube up and fuck different crevices all over his body (armpits, kneepits, valley between his pectorals).

- Lube both of your cocks and rub them together.
- 69, missionary position, doggy-style, "man on top."
- Make out while your dicks touch.
- Let him "discover" it in your pants or under your skirt.

Fun Things to Do When You're Fucking Him

- Pinch his nipples.
- Kiss him, intensely.
- Tell him how sexy he looks.
- Jack him off with each thrust.
- Spank his ass.
- Make him suck your fingers or nipples—or a second dildo.
- Have him jack himself off while you fuck him—two dicks at play.

The Feeldoe and Double Dildos

Here's a concept: How about strap-on sex, no harness required? The enterprising and pleasure-seeking woman-owned company Tantus (tantussilicone.com) thought long and hard (and long, and really hard...) to come up with a design for a dildo that can be worn by a female partner for hands-free penetration without a harness. They finally came up with what they call the Feeldoe. It really works, and there are legions of happy product testers behind (you might say) the final design they came up with, which is a bulb that fits snugly inside the vagina, with a right-angle penis-shaped shaft extending out the front. It comes in various sizes, it's made of silicone, and some models come with a vibrator at the base situated for clitoral stimulation during penetration.

The shaft is a nice smooth shape for anal penetration, as it's not contoured. The small one is my recommendation for novice ass-tronauts.

A double dildo crafted in a similar style, but created for use with or without a harness, is Vixen's Nexus, or its Nexus Jr. model. Vixen Creations (vixencreations.com) got tired of standard double dildos that are essentially a stick with two insertable ends, which are difficult to manipulate in tandem for orgasm. So they made a double that *really* works. The result,

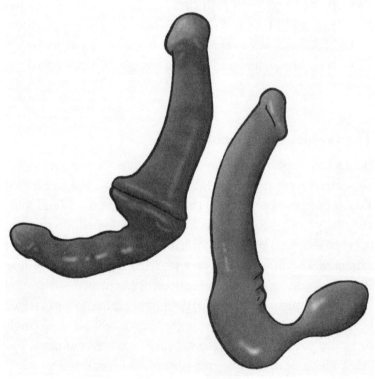

Illus. 10: Nexus and Feeldoe

Nexus, is a boomerang-shaped double made of silicone, with one shorter, slightly curved end, plus a longer, straighter end that allows both users to deliver true in-and-out motions. It also works well when worn in a harness (with a hole for insertion), letting both lovers enjoy more controlled penetration and thrusting. Some clever users have even used button-fly jeans instead of a harness with this versatile toy. Ride 'em, cowboy.

But how about those classic double dildos? They work great for penetration, and are an awful lot of fun to play with, even if they may not work as you'd expect for penetrative orgasms. But they don't work the way they do in porn movies, where they bring braying porn stars to screeching orgasms at the slightest pelvic thrust—they take a lot more coordination and communication than that to achieve success. But they're terrific for mutual masturbation with shared penetration, or for putting on jerk-off shows for each other while trying to keep the dildo in place. Their extra length makes double dildos excellent for people with limited mobility range. And all doubles, from the classics to the Feeldoe and the Nexus, can be enjoyed and used successfully (read: *get you off*) by couples.

Other Strap-Ons

You needn't limit your strap-on adventures to the standard variety of pubic protuberance. For instance, a thigh harness can make a lap dance or leg ride highly rewarding. Thigh harnesses either buckle onto your leg with a nylon strap or slide on by an elastic band. Some come with a dildo already seated in the strap-on, but the best version of this clever device has a hole or O-ring that enables you to swap dildos on a whim. Most of the nylon strap and buckle varieties have very long straps, which are great for big thighs but are often long enough to also fit around a waist (pony rides, anyone?), a pillow, a barstool, or any piece of furniture that happens to look at you with a "come hither" wink.

Face strap-ons are just that: a strap-on apparatus that buckles around the head to seat a dildo either right over the mouth of the wearer, or on the forehead. This type of strap-on effectively makes the wearer's head into a sex toy and provides a hell of a view for the harness wearer. Most have the dildo already attached, but try to find a head harness that allows you to use different dildos interchangeably so that you can use a dildo with the size and shape that you like, then after you've blasted off you can remove the dildo for thorough cleaning. People with neck or jaw injuries or whose neck muscles might strain easily will want to be a little more physically cautious and establish good communication with the person they're penetrating, as it's easy for someone near orgasm to buck a little too hard, or grab the head and thrust roughly. If you're worried about neck strain, lie flat with a pillow or two under your neck and head for cushioning, or experiment with the sex position pillows described in chapter 9, Sex Furniture.

Chapter 6

Teledildonic Toys: Online Sex for Two

We're on the verge of a sex and technology revolution. It's now possible to have sex with a lover thousands of miles away, by means of a computer interface. That's a sensational development, one that makes us appreciate new technologies with the zeal of a horny nerd. Right now two people (or more) can each turn on their computer, operate sex toys that are in another state or even country, and watch each other play—live and with few delays. Putting on a cam show in real time for your lover by computer has come a very long way in just the past few years. Sure, fantasies of *virtual reality* sex and ideas of cybersuits (where the wearer wouldn't even know the difference between a real sex partner and the virtual world in which they had the experiences and adventure) still remain in the realm of hoped-for fantasy for many, myself included. Yet right now, today, a wide variety of computer-controlled sex toys, remote-controlled interfaces, and even networks for meeting new cybersex partners let you have real and satisfying computer sex with your lover.

Teledildonics refers to sexual encounters via a Web interface with a virtual partner. The clever word (combining elements of *tele* [distant], *dildo*, and *electronics*) has become a catchall term for anything from virtual reality suits to remote-controlled vibrators. *Teledildonics* was coined in the 1980s by Ted Nelson, though the term is best associated with Howard Rheingold's 1991 book *Virtual Reality*. In a chapter entitled Teledildonics, Rheingold describes his fantasies of having virtual reality sex over the Internet, but wisely mentions the difficulties in making a virtual reality sex suit. Mind you, the Web wasn't actually usable for the general public until around 1993, but even when it only beckoned as a new frontier to those techies "in the know," it remained a fertile ground for sexual imagination.

Despite the squeaky-clean statistics you'll read in mainstream technology's industry reports, many important technological advances have been fueled by sex. Video rentals and the VHS videotape machine are two great examples, and it's certain that even if things like handicams, video podcasts, gallery websites, social networking sites, and a significant developmental portion of the Internet weren't precisely driven by sex, all of these technologies are intertwined with sex today like a pair of conjoined twins.

The interest in sex, and commercialized aspects of that pastime, have made these technologies widely popular and ushered them into mainstream usage. Sometimes, as with podcasting, it's the notion that the tech is pornified that garners it the headlines and leads the way for sexualization; it's arguable that podcasting hit the mainstream consciousness when the *Wall Street Journal* and *Newsweek* ran articles on "porn podcasts" even before video podcasting was accessible and at a time when only a handful of sex podcasts were available. After that came the developments and refinements in podcasting creation and delivery systems; it may be a "chicken or the egg?" debate in some circles, but it's obvious that both can't exist without each other—just as with tech development and sex. It may seem like Howard Rheingold's fantasies about virtual reality suits are light years behind us, but even if certain fantasies may not be feasible, many cybersex fantasies can come true with the click of a mouse in the Wild West frontier of—let's say it together— "teledildonic sex toys."

USB Sex Toys

The standard type of sex toy used for Internet-controlled sex is one that's USB-controlled, meaning that the toy has either been modified or manufactured with a USB cable or a remote (that is, wireless) USB transmitter. Every new computer has one or more USB ports; USB (Universal Serial Bus) is a plug-and-play interface between a computer and add-on devices (such as audio players, joysticks, keyboards, telephones, scanners, and printers). USB also acts as a power source for whatever you're using, so a USB sex toy never needs batteries. The types of sex toys fashioned into USB devices are typically the usual range of bullets, penis sleeves, and dual-action vibrators found at retail sex shops, the only difference being their USB power source.

Most sex toy retailers carry some kind of USB sex toy, but all of them are only *powered* by USB, meaning you still have a little controller box where you (manually) change the intensity of the vibrator; these toys can't be modified for computer control. They are handy for people who don't want to mess with batteries (and like the idea of alternate-powered toys) or want to have a toy every bit as mobile as their laptop. People with webcams love their USB sex toy, because it lets them put on relatively hassle-free sex shows for their lovers who are watching on the other end of the cam interface, whether across town or on the other side of the globe. Some USB sex toys are marketed and sold with (cheap and buggy) "3-D cyber sex games,"

Illus. 11: USB Vibe

a disc that runs porn or explicit sex games that power a penis stroker—buyer beware of what else might come on these discs, and don't expect nearly the level of graphics you get in a standard computer game like *Grand Theft Auto*. And don't *ever* buy a sex toy with claims of "optimizing your computer's performance" unless you know a lot about getting rooted spyware out of your hard drive.

Look sharp when purchasing a USB sex toy that doesn't include a teledildonic interface (only two companies provide these interfaces right now; they're explained in the next section). Almost all retailers, from the reputable to the sleazy, sell USB toys with the marketing text and descriptions promising "cybersex" and computer-controlled sex. These claims are untrue, though likely due to a lack of understanding of the toys themselves. As stated earlier, all USB sex toys are powered only by your computer; all the USB vibrators do is use the power coming *from* your computer the same as they would from a battery pack. There's no computer control for these toys, but what they're good for is powering a vibrator *while* you're having cybersex.

It's important to remember that because the ideas and technologies behind USB sex toys, teledildonics, and webcam interfaces are still evolving, they aren't without their drawbacks. So you'll need a realistic attitude when playing with USB-controlled sex toys and negotiating delays in image transmission because of your (or your lover's) slow Internet connection. Because teledildonics is still in its frontier stage of development, and will likely stay there for a while as different cowboy companies angle to devise the best toys and control programs, it's wise to remember that no interface will be entirely perfect for your cyberfantasies

Teledildonic USB Sex Toys

Two companies sell USB-powered sex toys that can be used over the Internet with a lover (or stranger, if you prefer). Both Sinulate Entertainment and HighJoy Products market a selection of USB sex toys with proprietary software that allows for remote Web control of the toys. Sinulate sells its toys with software that the user installs on their computer, and offers a free network interface where users register their toys for enjoyment with a remote user. HighJoy, by contrast, sells a subscription service for remote use of its USB toys. Both companies offer a network of "singles," pay-for-play cam girl-shows, and "interactive 3-D sex fantasy games." Neither company, alas, offers options for Macintosh users.

Over at sinulate.com, the Sinulator uses a Flash interface point-and-click control panel that lets users of the Sinulate system and software operate toys via the Internet. A vibrator attaches to a wireless transmitter by a short cord, while another wireless transmitter connects to the user's PC through a USB port. Each toy gets a unique user name and URL, which is what's registered in the online remote-user network. Then the toy owner

---

No Teledildonics for Mac Users

Unfortunately, to date no teledildonic service offers Mac-compatible software—yet. This is a shameful state that all sexy Apple computer users must deplore, and a sad commentary on the lack of imagination of the teledildonics industry. So, speaking as one horny Mac user to all randy and computer-savvy readers, I say it's high time we create open-source, nonproprietary teledildonics—it'll surely make a better world for everyone.

gives the user name and URL to the person they want to have control the toy. The operator controls the toy from the Sinulator-hosted webpage of the person with the Sinulator toy, and pilots the toy's intensity by clicking and dragging their mouse by means of the Flash interface. If the toy user has a webcam set up, the remote operator can watch the results onscreen.

The Sinulator claims wireless capabilities of up to 50 feet from the transmitter, so toy users have the freedom of masturbatory mobility and no wires to get tangled in. That means the person using the toy can recline on a couch or bed away from the computer and talk on their cell phone with a lover running the sex toy, or if they're more ambitious they can set up a little webcam studio for an elaborate scene. The Flash interface resembles an adolescent boy's idea of an airline cockpit, which operates a Rabbit Habit (dual-action) vibrator in a variety of ways, with a throttle (rotate), slider (vibrate), and three buttons that execute combined rotation and vibration programs.

Sinulator's interface works like a video game, except that the operator can run the vibrator on any Internet-connected device containing a browser, such as a Treo, to control the Sinulator vibe used by a woman or man, anywhere. The inventors cleverly created a hidden control panel for the person on the vibrating end of the deal, where he or she can limit the intensity of the vibrator—so while their client or lover is maxing out the rotate function (thinking that more must be better), the person with the vibe receives only the level of rotation that they find pleasurable. A true win–win situation.

Flash technology, which adds animation and interactivity to webpages, gives users spontaneous opportunities to play with the interface, though Flash has its own quirks and problems with different computer models and browser types. The receiver box arrives in a tasteful pillow with a simple quick-start guide (supplemented by a detailed start-up brochure). The USB connection both powers and connects the transmitter; the Sinulator is FCC compliant.

The Sinulator is not Mac compatible on the user end; the toy operator can be on any computer, though the toy user is limited to a PC only.

Over at highjoy.com, the HighJoy Products system promises services similar to those of the Sinulator, and the company has merged it with a membership-required, highly proprietary, social networking/dating service–style website. The company's base setup starts at over a hundred dollars, plus a required monthly membership fee. System requirements are Windows 98 SE or later, an Internet connection, and either a serial port (COM port) or a USB port (a serial-to-USB adapter is sold separately).

HighJoy has partnered with novelty toy manufacturers Doc Johnson and the Vivid porn company. Three toys, two webcams, lubes, and two adaptors are offered in their online store. The site is based on a social networking model, encouraging users to sign up and create profiles so they can meet other users and have sex with them. Like a commercial social networking site, the partnership collects data on users: all personal information, all user profile information, computer information, IP address, browser type, domain names, access times, referrers, and specific pages visited.

Buyer beware: HighJoy's privacy policy states that "HJP may use this data to deliver customized content and advertising to customers whose behavior indicates that they are interested in a particular subject area.... HJP also uses your personal information to inform you of other products or services available from HJP and its affiliates. HJP may also contact you via surveys." While it claims not to sell your info to third parties, it may try to sell you products of external business partners. So it's a good idea, as always with online purchases, to print a copy of the license agreement and read it before signing up.

Set Up a Webcam

You don't need to pay for an expensive cybersex USB toy serv- ice to enjoy the many pleasures of having live, remote sex with someone over the Web. You can do this with a webcam. Granted, it may not fulfill the complete fantasy of having a lover control your toy, but a little visual stimulation can go a long way, and controlling your own orgasmic destiny gives you a lot of advan- tages. Think about it: In any remote Web sex encounter, you're essentially just masturbating and talking dirty together anyway—you're not touching, or breathing heavily into some- one's ear. Shared sex is all in the eye (and the ear) of the beholder. But before you decide who's calling the shots and controlling the encounter, and whether you want to move up to try remote sex toys, just get a camera set up and ready to go.

Essentially, setting up a webcam can be as easy as purchas- ing it, installing the software that comes with it, and following the directions for use. Make sure you read the instructions before plugging in the camera. Some require that you install the driv- ers first; others require the camera to be plugged in first. If you do it in the wrong order, you may not be able to get the camera working at all. Don't even bother with a webcam if your Internet connection is dial-up; it will simply be too slow and unreliable for practical sexual use.

Webcams sit on, and plug into, your computer for Web use; most webcams come with microphones that let you talk and transmit sound to and from the person you're connected with. How much you spend on this equipment is up to you and, while quality varies widely, most consumer ratings websites agree that, as in all things technological, you get what you pay for.

Illus. 12: Webcam

High-end webcams come with flattering features, such as lighting adjustment and instant "enhancing" features like wrinkle smoothing and vertical stretching (to make you look thinner).

You have two basic choices when deciding how to get your images to your sweetie. Most people use IM (instant messaging) chat services because they're the easiest, and the most private. Practically all IM services, such as Yahoo, AIM, Skype, and iChat, have webcam capabilities; all you'll need is a camera and an account, and for your lover to have an account with the same service.

The other option is to host the image on your website, using webcam software that uploads the camera's images in intervals called "refresh rates." This is more complicated than using an IM interface, and privacy is an obvious issue, unless you already run a pay site or are familiar enough with hiding URLs or creating password-protected areas on your website. With this method, once your webcam is installed and configured, you'll need to set up the FTP (file transfer protocol) within the webcam software. Depending on the software, you may need to build and put in place a webpage to contain your webcam image. Some webcam programs come with built-in webpage builders but others don't, so keep this in mind before you purchase a webcam package if that's what you're shopping for.

It's not as simple as slapping up a new page on your website; you actually need to encode parameters to make the image on the page the same size as what the camera is sending. See what size image your camera snaps, and use that in the HTML; don't resize your camera images with the HTML, as this will distort the image and make it grainy (or grainier). You'll also need to "tell" the page that it must refresh the image automatically. so that your viewers get a new image every few seconds.

In the ‹head› of your HTML document, place the following two lines:

```
‹meta http-equiv="refresh" content="30" /›
‹meta http-equiv="expires" content="0" /›
```

In the "refresh" meta tag, if you want your page to refresh less (or more) often than every 30 seconds, change the content="30" to something other than 30, such as 60 (1 minute), 300 (5 minutes), or whatever you prefer. The "expires" tag is essential, as it affects the cache of Web browsers, so that the page isn't cached but rather pulled new from the server on every load.

Tips for a Sexy Webcam Show

Generally, flattering views can be achieved by placing your webcam above your eye level—anything lower will make you look like you have a double chin. Also, angling the camera off to the side will have you angling your head a bit when you face the camera—a pinup modeling trick for flattering facial angles. A full-on face shot makes for a round face. It's usually more flattering to turn to a slight angle. Learn how your face looks from a profile to a full-face shot and all the angles in between. A good standard angle is a 3/4 shot, with both eyes visible to the camera. Of course, you may not care to have your face star in your cam show at all; you can keep the camera aimed at breasts (for this, a lower angle is more flattering, to provide a view upward at the breasts), or just at the main area of action, the genitals. Move the hips one way, the shoulders the other, and tilt the head. Think of swaying lines running down through

Pinup Posing Tips

The pros do it, too: Look at magazines and pictures for poses you like, then practice them in a mirror. Have your shoulders on an angle, and tilt your head toward your near shoulder. For body shots, keep your shoulders square and angle your hips for a slimming effect. Keep your back straight and always remind yourself to stick out your chest, to avoid slumping. And if you wear makeup, apply more than normal.

your body. This gives pleasing lines for the eye to follow in the image you're sending.

In your webcam shows, lighting is extremely important, though you don't have to go crazy emptying your wallet on fancy lights to get great results. Misplaced lights will get you hard shadows that can accentuate tired eyes, or any other bits that you'd rather looked perkier. Avoid the unflattering, scary shadows of direct overhead light, or light coming from beneath you, and never use fluorescent lighting, which causes ghastly, "undead" coloring in even the healthiest cybersexual. Unless it's a Halloween show, of course—then do everything I'm telling you *not* to do, and you'll achieve the dramatic zombie look of lust you've always dreamed of. The flicker and glow of your computer monitor might be the mood you want to set, though keep in mind that whatever color is on your screen (backgrounds, an IM page) is what will be lighting your show.

Webcams, by their technical limitations, look grainy, and poor lighting can make your images look even more distorted. Experiment with lighting styles and angles as you view yourself onscreen; move your light around, or buy a clip-on lamp that can be positioned as you please. Warmer lighting will come from halogen bulbs, which closely mimic natural light. I highly recommend using natural light whenever possible. If you want to add the illusion of depth, use a three-point lighting system (this can easily be done with household lamps), where there's one primary bright light, a softer light coming from the opposite side, then a back light to enhance your shape as the subject and bring you out from the background. Remember that your monitor will always add light right in front of your face, and experiment with colored bulbs in lamps for mood and effect.

Your Very Own Cam Show

Even if your directorial ambition is just to have a camera pointed at your crotch, you'll want to avoid the frustrations of having to get up and hunt for that special dildo at a crucial moment. Get your great toys ready before you start your cam date. Assemble a near-off-camera location for all the toys you think you'll want to play with, and don't forget the lube, check all battery toys to make sure they function, and have a towel or Handi Wipes ready in case you need to adjust the camera or settings midshow.

Get yourself ready, too. Take a relaxing bath or shower beforehand, listen to music that puts you in the mood, watch a little porn, or even feel free to masturbate awhile before you go live— the better to get yourself really turned on. Have your camera all set up and lighting in place, be sure that the room is heated and that you'll have no distractions or interruptions from cell phones, other chat software or email alerts, or roommates. Adjust the screensaver and sleep functions on your computer so they don't activate at the wrong moment—think how sad it would be to miss part of your lover's orgasm because your dancing polar bears screensaver went on right as your lover came.

You can get as creative as you like with your background, props, and outfits. Drape a red satin sheet over your office chair, take your laptop and webcam to bed, buy a faux-fur throw at a thrift store and recline on it like a centerfold. Hang a nice (unwrinkled) sheet behind you for a plain or colored background, or give yourself nerdy flair by propping yourself on pillows in front of a bookcase. Incorporate slinky nightgowns or marabou-trimmed robes or feather boas. Wear sexy lingerie, nothing at all, or your everyday clothes to strip out of as things heat up while you chat. You can get really imaginative or kinky and wear a nurse or schoolgirl outfit, formal wear, a corporate suit, a strap-on dildo, bondage or BDSM items (which you can safely get out of); you can even dress in layers for a cam show striptease. You can let your lover direct the scene, or you can take firm control of what they get, teasing and turning them on as you slowly peel your clothes off and touch yourself as they only *wish* they could, and slowly massaging oil or lotion into your skin (or lube on your genitals) while they watch. After that, the fantasy is up to both of you!

Chapter 7

Sex Machines

Depending on your point of view, a sex machine is any mechanical apparatus used to stimulate the genitalia, a nickname for a tireless body part, a song by James Brown, or even the character played by Tom Savini in the cult vampire movie *From Dusk Till Dawn*. And while you and your lover can watch the movie with the sound turned down so you can hear the song while you go at it like a couple of machines, having an *actual* sex machine in the room for you to play with can turn an evening of sex into an endless session of orgasmic endeavors—because the sex machine itself is truly tireless.

And that's part of the appeal of a sex machine. By today's definition, a sex machine is a large device that vibrates or penetrates the user, or both, powered by electricity. These simple machines all perform pretty simple tasks: They buzz, they go in-and-out, or they spin a dildo—tirelessly. They're often so big that the user sits astride the machine like riding a mechanical bull, or position their body on the large and imposing, and often loud, mechanical device—which is all part of the appeal. Sex machines are the ultimate crossroad where vulnerable human interaction and intimacy says hello to a cold, powerful, mechanical device. By sexualizing the machine in these fucking-machine interactions, we even give the machine an anthropomorphic quality, teasing ourselves for our own perceptions about machines and robots having lives and personalities. By having sex with a machine, a woman can be seen as either conquering or being conquered by a powerful and imposing sex toy. Either way she slices it, sex machines represent to her the ultimate tireless lover, able to deliver satisfaction long after other human beings wear out.

The iconic sex machines website is FuckingMachines.com, a professionally produced porn site that features amateur men and women having sex with a wide variety of machines. Some are very crude and homemade looking—like a kitchen appliance modified with a dildo attachment—while others are huge and complex, calling up images from science fiction movies. Sex machine fantasies run this range, from the homemade "drilldo" (a drill-dildo hybrid) to fantastic and imposing machines. They have hot contemporary competition in the form of sites such as Machine Maidens (machinemaidens.com), where you can see a variety of machines at work and can evaluate your shopping checklist. Fucking Machines put machine sex on the map and into the popular consciousness, paving the way for a few individual companies to mass produce somewhat affordable sex machines that couples and individuals can purchase and use at home.

You can find a huge sex machine subculture of individual and independent inventors online in social networking sites, chat groups, and listservs dedicated to makers of amateur sex

---

Sex Machine Manufacturers

Some of the best manufacturers of sex machines on the market today are the Sybian (sybian.com), the Monkey Rocker (monkeyrocker.com; see more information in chapter 9, Sex Furniture), the Thethrillhammer (thethrillhammer.com), and Thepowerpulse (thepowerpulse.com). Also visit the websites of Orgasm Alley (orgasmalley.com) and Ken's Twisted Mind (kenstwistedmind.com).

---

machines. But if you want a sex machine to use at home, and don't care to strip down your nice KitchenAid mixer to epoxy a dildo onto it, you have a few options. Just make sure you buy your sex machine direct from the manufacturer, rather than from a sex toy retail giant, to ensure that you're not getting a knock-off—unless you're certain the retailer is reputable and you've ordered from it before.

Ken's Twisted Mind (KTM Enterprises)

No one has a bigger or better selection of a jaw-dropping variety of sex machines than Ken's Twisted Mind (kenstwistedmind.com). This is the Home Depot of sex toys sites: It has all the basics, an enormous range of models and styles, and tips on building your own. Most of the machines are of the in-and-out repetitive variety, but they come in so many shapes, heights, and configurations that it's mind-boggling. For instance, the Furniture Mate is a thrusting machine situated on a stable stand that can be adjusted for slant and height to penetrate at the desired angle while situated on any piece of furniture, while the Bed Buddy comes on an L-shaped stand to penetrate on the same level plane as the user (as on a bed, for example).

The machines here range from the simplistic power-tool variety all the way to extravagant, handheld-cabled machines in aluminum cases that cost well over a thousand dollars. The site is available in Spanish, French, German, Italian, and Portuguese, and Ken ships worldwide. A lengthy buyer's guide page explains the warranties (2 to 10 years) and defines terminology such as *stroke length* (pretty much what it sounds like). KTM also features a variety of toys for men that utilize men's masturbation sleeves and toys such as the Fleshlight, making them into robotic masturbation devices.

All of Ken's Twisted Mind penetration sex machines use sex toy novelty manufacturer Doc Johnson's Vac-U-Lock dildos and system for attachment. A wide variety of dildos and vibrators is available to use with this system (which is basically a dildo with a hole in it that suctions onto a ribbed peg with silicone powder "lubricant"); it's a very secure way to attach the dildos to the machines. But the problem is that the company's dildos are only available in unhygienic, porous materials—unfortunately, that means latex, jelly rubber, and mystery composite materials (see chapter 1, Basic Models, and Care and Feeding of Your Toys, for more information on the care and cleaning of these materials). Still, Doc Johnson's toys are inexpensive and easy to come by at almost any sex toy retailer. While Ken's Twisted Mind makes high-quality sex machines and has an excellent privacy policy, all the dildos and toys that attach to the machines come with a caveat: "The items offered for sale on and through this website are sold as novelties and collector's items."

Sybian

Of all the sex machines widely available to consumers, the Sybian (sybian.com) is the most popular and widely recognized of them all, perhaps due to its starring role in a significant number of porn films and its use on a variety of adult websites. It's also an extremely popular machine in the swinging lifestyle (or sub-culture) and regularly appears as a guest of honor at sex parties.

Looking like the top half of a mechanical bull, the Sybian is shaped like a wide motorcycle seat with a flat base so that the user rides it, or sits astride the machine. It's a fairly large and heavy machine, at 13"x10"x10" and 22 pounds, and the rider needn't worry about it actually moving while in use. It's also (allegedly) rated to withstand 1,000 pounds. The Sybian is covered in padded black Naugahyde, with the attachments in beige "flesh" tone. The area that does all the work is situated right at the seat's apex; where the rider's genitals make contact, a vibrating area stimulates a number of optional attachments. There's no in-and-out thrusting by this machine, but instead it gives intense, variable-speed vibrations or rotating action to attachments that range from a "flat" dildo to dildos of different sizes, and even a double penetration attachment. The user can sit in place, "ride" the machine, or wiggle around all he or she likes.

The Sybian runs on standard U.S. 120v current and also has a 240v version for worldwide use; it simply plugs into the wall socket and you're ready to go. A cable extends from the machine, connecting a very basic control box that controls vibration intensity and rotation. It's a quite loud machine and not recommended if you have concerns about noise, though one solution is to place the machine on a padded surface like a bed or cushion to absorb the loud motor sounds.

The Sybian's attachments are made of rubber—sadly, they're not made of hygienic silicone, so extra steps will need to be taken to ensure cleanliness. Rubber can't be sterilized, so it's not recommended that you share this machine unless you've cleaned the machine and toys with bacteria-killing agents. The attachments can withstand a run through the dishwasher on the top rack for a full cycle, though, unlike silicone, they can't be boiled. To clean between uses, wash with a fragrance-free antibacterial soap like Hibiclens or a 1:10 bleach and water solution,

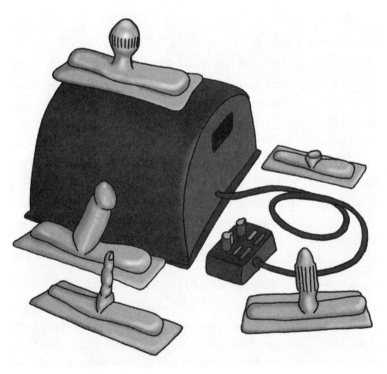

Illus 13: Sybian

followed by detergent (dish soap) and a hot water rinse. Allow the attachments to dry completely before use; when in doubt about insertion attachments, use a condom on them and be sure the surface of the Sybian has been wiped down with a sterile towelette or solution. The Sybian sells a novelty-manufactured "toy cleaner" as the recommended cleaner—though it's nothing more than dish soap with the ingredient Nonoxynol-9 (an irritating detergent that's been shown to cause cervical abrasions when used in lubricants, and kills HIV/AIDS only in clinical settings).

If you're not sharing your Sybian, this is less of an issue. You can just wash its attachments with soap and water for a few uses, sterilizing them completely every fourth or fifth use and being sure to follow the common sense guidelines for sex toys and anal use in chapter 1. Beware of cheaply made Sybian look-alikes that have poorly made attachments (typically unhygienic jelly rubber) and a motor that burns out or can't withstand regular use. The legitimate Sybian model comes with a five-year warranty, the shipping is discreet, and the company has a good privacy policy—but at more than a thousand dollars for a complete Sybian package with attachments, it's an investment that should come with *some* kind of guarantee.

Roll Your Own Sex Machines?

Whether you want to save money or make your dream machine, building your own fuck machine is no small project. You'll need a basic knowledge of mechanics and motors, skill with household wiring, and familiarity with aspects of sex toys such as how they deliver pleasure to the user and how you can keep everything on them clean.

Ways Two Can Play on a Sex Machine

- Watch porn together while using the machine.
- Just watch your lover have fun with the machine.
- One receives oral sex (standing in front) while the other rides.
- Take turns with the controls.
- One rides, the other fondles and plays with the rider.
- Get kinky: The rider gets handcuffed, or arms are bound.
- Blindfold the rider and surprise them with squeezes, spanks, feathers, or more.

So the Sybian is popular, even though it is somewhat clunky, and the claims about women and orgasm on the company's website are a little dated...but does it work? Most certainly. The Sybian is a swingers' party favor and a porn star for a good reason: It delivers strong, consistent stimulation; it's easily controllable by the user for getting "just right" stimulation at precisely the right times; and it's comfortable to sit on. It's often seen in female masturbation porn films where the orgasms (for once) are authentic. The Sybian has a well-earned reputation for excellent G-spot stimulation and for producing terrific results in female ejaculation. For couples, the Sybian offers lots of play options, most notably in situations where one player just wants to watch, where lovers want to trade use of the controls, or where the rider wants to perform oral sex on their lover while riding. In power exchange scenarios, the machine can be used as an instrument of both pleasure and punishment, when one of the partners is "made" to stay on the machine.

The Sybian company also sells a sex machine for men called the Venus 2000, an electricity-powered stroker with variable-speed vibration and stroke controls. It's basically an 11-pound black box that the penis goes into, where inside it's surrounded by a rubber liner and machinery that tugs, sucks, strokes, and vibrates the penis. There are some pretty funny claims on the website about how the machine creates erections, "trains" against premature ejaculation, and "Maintains Penial Health" (sic), which should all be taken with a good-natured grain of salt. A variety of inserts and attachments is available.

Thethrillhammer and Thepowerpulse

Over at thethrillhammer.com and thepowerpulse.com, Daphna and Allen Stein have worked with a team of twelve engineers and roboticists, as well as with the folks at Sybian (sybian.com) and Advanced Medical Robotics (erotichine.com), to make Thethrillhammer and Thepowerpulse. Both machines are designed to appeal to an exclusive clientele, are highly stylish, and look as if they arrived from the future on a UFO—though in fact both are thoughtfully designed sex machines created specifically to give women sexual thrills.

Thethrillhammer is a big, expensive, imposing-looking machine that the user gets into, rather than sits on, and is the most exclusive of all the sex machines; each machine is tailor-made for the individual customer. It is a giant, sci-fi-looking adjustable chair that's a cross between a dentist's chair and a gynecological exam table. In its most basic incarnation the machine includes a thrustable, rotating, and vibrating dildo, plus a controllable webcam—the machine can be used over the Web with

Thethrillhammer's Flash interface. It's quite simply the world's first Web-controlled sex machine.

To ride the machine, the user relaxes into the chair while an operator employs the functions of "thrust," "rotate," "vibrate," "camera zoom, tilt, pan," and advanced options such as preset patterns. The control interface is Flash, so it can be operated from any computer or operating system that has a browser. As with the Sinulator, end users can control the maximum amount

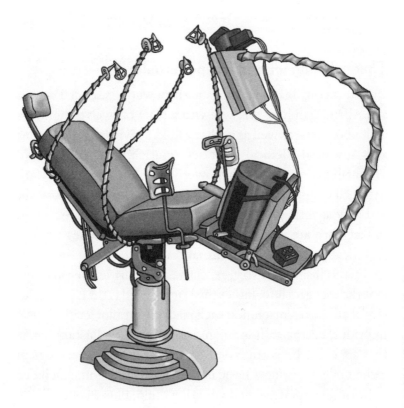

Illus. 14: Thethrillhammer

Sex Machines, the Book

If you're more interested in the sex machine subculture, pick up a copy of *Sex Machines: Photographs and Interviews*, by Timothy Archibald. See the amazing photos and read the results of photographer Archibald's journey around the United States researching and documenting sex machine culture, from the big-business manufacturers to the sex machine hobbyist.

of stimulation so they can still enjoy a pleasurable low volume of vibration, thrust, or rotation, while the person doing the controlling can get their rocks off by jamming the volume up to the max.

Thethrillhammer consumer models (most are for commercial porn use) are described as "custom machines for kinky people who might also have a medical fetish" and sell to a high-end sex toy market of private clients. Indeed, their roboticist hails from making machines for the sophisticated tastes of House of Gord, "The home of ultra-bondage...the ultimate in restraint, trussing, cocooning, human furniture, packaged girls and suspension" (houseofgord.com). Estimates for custom machines start at more than $4,000; they can be modified with virtually "anything the client desires."

On the retail end, this is an exclusive machine for people with money—and that's fine with the Steins. "Sinulate has the commodity end of the market nailed," they said in an interview; "we want to complement them and appeal to the individual buyers who want a tailored experience, and businesses that want to offer something more to their clients." Thethrillhammer has a similar nonadult background as Sinulate Entertainment, and both companies are friendly entrepreneurs looking toward their shared future in the teledildonics field, pushing for standardization in Web-controlled sex toys. For now, setup is limited to custom installation, though clients run Thethrillhammer smoothly on their own after startup. An air compressor supplies the rhythm, so noise is a consideration, yet the entire unit is powered on regular electricity.

Thepowerpulse is marketed as a "luxury sex machine" and, at a glance, this is, without a doubt, true. Designed by an artist and fabricated by the woman-owned and operated Thethrillhammer team, it's a gorgeous piece of artwork that looks like it should be either in a design museum or on a spaceship's pleasure deck. Brushed aluminum and stainless steel are the signature of this machine, which delivers an in-and-out thrust of up to 250 strokes per minute, has variable-speed vibration, is quiet and runs on standard wall-socket electricity, and in addition to extralong power cords, also has a wireless remote control. It stands on its own adjustable four feet, uses the Doc Johnson Vac-U-Loc system for dildo and vibrator attachment, and retails for about two thousand dollars.

Chapter 8

Exotic Sex Toys

If you're the kind of person who thinks that life's pleasures should be a decadent indulgence to be truly appreciated, you're not alone. While the rest of the sex toy business has been churning out the cheapest products made from disposable materials, a growing number of naughty entrepreneurs have taken on a different perspective altogether, creating super-exquisite haute couture sex toys. Many new toy manufacturers want to distance themselves from "novelties" as much as possible, and often have backgrounds in engineering, design, and art. Welcome to the wonderful and fast-growing world of highly refined pleasure instruments.

Whether you think "only the best will do" for your sexual escapades, or you see yourself as needing a solid rose quartz dildo reposing in an exquisite locked box on your bedside table, or you're a couple whose fantasies only begin in vistas of decadence that require the proper accessories, or you want to get your lover the most mind-blowing sexy gift imaginable, there's likely a high-end sex toy to fulfill your desires. If you can imagine it, it's probably available—though not without a hefty price tag (of course). Yet for people who want their sex toys ringed with real diamonds and gleaming with personalized monograms, money isn't the object: Pleasure is.

While in the rest of the sex toy world, silicone is the expensive, most-desired material available, in the world of high-end sex toys you can find playthings crafted from exotic materials like steel, silver, platinum, gold, glass/Pyrex, and wood, or even carved from precious stones. Anal beads made from freshwater pearls? No problem. Real fox-fur tails for your butt plug? Sad for the fox, but available with the click of a mouse for your foxy little ass.

Glass and Pyrex Sex Toys

Toys made of glass and Pyrex look and feel incredible—and as for an extravagant plaything, they've got the form and function part down pat, too. Looking more like modern sculptures or works of art you can hold in your hand, glass toys are perfectly fashioned into ultrasmooth and deliciously heavy sex toys. Glass sex toys might make you feel as if you're "living on the edge" as far as breakage goes, but in fact these toys are crafted with an advanced process that makes them incredibly difficult to break—and no orifice of yours has the power to break them. Of course, if you drop them on a hard surface or they knock against each other, you might need a new glass toy. But they're amazingly resilient, and should be, after going through heat-curing processes averaging 5,000 degrees Fahrenheit.

Glass toys are readily available through a variety of retailers, and for value, you get what you pay for; expect prices of up to $400. Glass toys come in all shapes, from small butt plugs to far-out curved alien penetration toys, solid glass police night-sticks (the "Night Shift" at blowfish.com), and outrageous things like "The Juicer," a glass insertion toy with a hand-crank handle that lets you rotate the toy inside someone, literally like turning a winch. Another exciting creation is the Black Light Responsive glass dildo, an amazing-looking creation that safely holds a suspended liquid inside that refracts and glows under a black light. All glass toys are clear and made from hearty stuff,

Illus. 15: Exotic Toys

and many have ribbons of color that catch and refract light at different angles. This makes each and every glass toy a unique creation, no two alike.

By far the most discriminating glass creations are from Clear Ecstasy (clearecstasy.com). This company takes its self-pleasure (and its glass) seriously, coming up with some of the more outrageous glass toys in existence. There you can find a variety of glass toys (like the aforementioned "Juicer") and, time and money allowing, you can even have the company create a custom glass dildo for you. The "Don Wand" is its version of a make-a-dildo, though in stunning glass and with a variety of customizable options. For instance, you can simply have a glass dildo made to your size and shape specs, or go the distance and opt to add colors, internal monograms (cost is per letter), embedded quartz crystals, opals, Herkimer (quartz that simulates a diamond), or dichromate chips (iridescent diachronic glass chips). Clear Ecstasy also proffers the "thousand dollar dildo," called The Venis: a gorgeous, handcrafted glass dildo whose handle resembles a female torso.

Heavy Metals, Stone, and Precious Gems

Like glass, metal dildos and butt plugs are perfectly smooth and wonderfully heavy, making them ideal for G-spot and prostate play. Stainless steel sex toys are widely available at retailers that specialize in kinky toys (such as stockroom.com and blowfish.com); they come with a fat price tag and range from basic shapes and designs to outrageous creations with huge jewels and gems embedded in them, handles to simulate Baroque door-knockers, and Chinese dragon heads; some even have fanciful (or frightening)

Hot and Cold Running Sex Toys

As you might imagine, glass and metal toys feel cold and smooth, yet they warm up nicely and retain heat well. Some people like to make them even cooler—or hotter—for intense temperature play. Never freeze or boil glass or metal, as you'll harm the integrity of the toy and harm the user's sensitive skin. Instead, warm these toys in hot tap water for a few minutes, or dip them in ice water.

---

faces cast into the handles. Metal toys are made of stainless steel on metal lathes, which spin the metal at mind-boggling speeds to remove material in precise measurements, and then are finished to create a perfectly smooth, seamless, nonporous surface. Aluminum sex toys are out there but difficult to find and expensive, as their material is very valuable in large chunks.

Few metal dildos come in traditional penis shapes; mostly you'll find sleek silver wands with a bulbous, perfectly round ball at the end, "barbell" shaped wands, and heavy, simple rods with ridges. Metal butt plugs come in standard (and even extra-large) shapes and some dastardly looking anal-bead-style graduated plugs, but the main differences are in how the base is finished—with a gem, a cast metal face or even a skull, a movable ring that acts as an extra handle, and more. Because metal is so strong, manufacturers can craft a variety of shapes and items, knowing that the items can withstand all sorts of play. More unusual metal sex toys include an aluminum "tuning fork" suitable for double penetration, a steel "vagina hook" for use in BDSM and intense bondage play, and bondage devices like a "nose hook," used to hold the head at a certain angle during bondage play.

For top-of-the line metal insertables that excel in form and function, point your browser to njoytoys.com. Njoy Toys's finely crafted beauties were conceived by a fellow with a background in the engineering and design of consumer products. Suitably for toys that will help you blast off, they're fabricated in a facility that also manufactures aerospace components. These toys impart equal amounts of beauty, thoughtful design for use, and an understanding of the pleasure potential in stainless steel. Expect to pay at least a hundred dollars for one of Njoy's stunning Philippe Starck–looking sex toys, and know that you're getting something worth way, way more.

Like glass and metal sex toys, stone dildos and butt plugs provide weight, smoothness, and temperature transmission (and retention) like no ordinary sex toy—but with the added delight of being shaped purely for pleasure from elements formerly deep within the earth. Stone dildos, available in kink-friendly and upscale sex toy boutiques, are typically made from a smooth, highly polished black (or dark green) granite; the result looks like a museum-quality work of art, or maybe what we might imagine dildos were like thousands of years ago—at least, the ones treasured by kings and queens. Granite dildos are either representational (they look like a penis) or shaped like wands with gently undulating waves for extra sensation, while granite butt plugs come in plain plug shapes. Because granite is stone and prone to lose its strength when drilled or decorated, it's uncommon to find anything other than smooth polished granite toys in classic designs.

One company has taken the notion of dildos and butt plugs in precious materials to the limit: Mi-Su (mi-su.com) is a U.K.-based company that retails very few items, but the ones it does sell are right at the edge of sexual decadence. At Mi-Su, you can get stunning butt plugs in obsidian or rose quartz that resemble chess pieces, or a nonrepresentational, sumptuously curved obsidian dildo. The same dildo is available in solid titanium and finished in a variety of colors, with a handle that can be custom inlaid with a selection of twenty precious stones, including diamonds and sapphires (or Swarovski crystals). Not wanting anyone to feel left out, Mi-Su also has a line of titanium cock rings in solid and adjustable styles; these are customizable with engravings, plus inlaid diamonds, rubies, or any precious gem that tickles a gentleman's fancy.

Not to be outdone, Coco de Mer (coco-de-mer.co.uk), an online sex boutique in London, offers a full line of wonderfully debauched sex toys crafted from truly exclusive materials. Even if decadent window shopping is all you can afford, visit its online store and check out the black glass-and-silver dildo; cock rings, butt plug, and dildo hand-carved from jade; and ingenious anal beads and cock rings in freshwater pearl. Keep looking, and you'll find a diamante-encrusted handle and leather whip named the Diva, and another whip called the Bombshell, whose tails are 100 percent human hair (available in blonde, redhead, or brunette). Kinky big spenders should match the Diva whip with a diamante and leather T-Shaped Strap with Detachable Cuffs (a stunning body harness), or the pony fetishist's dream: the leather corset Horse Tail Belt, made with real horse hair.

Specialty Vibrators

To appreciate just how technologically advanced that a money-is-no-object vibrator can be, look no further than the Je Joue

Programmable Vibrator (jejoue.com). This sexy little gadget uses a USB connection to download "grooves" that the Je Joue can later play back while the device snuggles up to your clit. It comes with 10 grooves preprogrammed, and, with its PleasureWare software, allows users to create, edit, and even share custom programs, which can last up to 30 minutes each. Once programmed or downloaded, grooves are transferred to Je Joue via USB. The website has an online groove-share directory, where users can upload and share their favorite grooves; so if you're not feeling inspired, you can try someone else's groove. Grooves can also be emailed.

London-based designer Shiri Zinn's Minx Vibrator (shirizinn.com) is an outrageous work of art that comes in its own satin-lined snakeskin box, just begging for display. If you don't wear fur, you'll want to skip this one, but if you have no problem with animal products then this fox-tailed (or feathered) vibe will be right at home between your thighs. Made of high-quality pink acrylic, it features 12 pink Swarovski crystals and a stainless steel end cap with detachable fox-fur tail (or feathers). It even comes with its own silver engraved stand.

Looking for ergonomics mixed with feminine beauty in a truly high-end vibe? Lelo (lelousa.com) has an entire line of gently curved, nonrepresentational, rechargeable vibrators—sold as "pleasure objects"—that have silky-smooth surfaces and near-silent vibrations. These toys don't look anything like vibrators but, with their sleek shapes and delicately engraved white flowers, they more resemble glossy, Japanese-inspired porcelain collectibles. The top of the line is Lelo's 18-karat gold-plated Yva Vibrator. Each comes in its own satin pouch with a wooden gift box, one-year warranty, and universal charger. How exquisite is that?!

Elemental Pleasures (elementalpleasures.com) is where the design and craftsmanship of Njoy's stainless steel aerospace metal toys meets the desire to make them into vibrators. Elemental's line of "luxury vibrators" encompasses one central style of metal vibrator available in stainless steel, anodized aluminum in three colors, and titanium—yes, titanium. That's Le Lynx, a hypoallergenic, medical-grade, silver titanium vibrator that comes in its own lockable attaché case. Each vibe ships with three tips that change the vibrational speed; it's incredibly quiet, is presented in its own locking metal case, and, unlike all other high-end vibes, can be used in water and therefore can be boiled, for complete sterilization.

Exotic Dildos

Whenever we think of dildos (for some of us that's often), we tend to visualize classic, rubbery, penis-shaped shafts that vaguely resemble something that might attach to a human body, or at least to a Ken-doll's body if it were somehow transmuted into a life-sized specimen. But not all of us are content to play with the parts that come stock, or even as add-on accessories, and quite a few of us want to play with sex toys that are out there even beyond the strange imaginings of designers at novelty sex toy companies. It's interesting to note, too, that the companies that have created a full line of dildos in the shapes of alien penises, animal penises, and even religious icons have chosen to do so with 100 percent silicone, the completely hygienic, sterilizable sex toy material. So weird, maybe; unsettling, sometimes; but sophisticated?—definitely.

London-based Alien Dildos (aliendildos.com) is especially proud that its toys are made from high-quality silicone, even if they look like something that truly belongs on ET. Each bizarrely bumpy, yet erotically compelling otherworldly penis is handcrafted (there's a two-week wait while they make your far-out dick—now *there's* a job you can wrap your mind around), comes in over a dozen colors, and is thoughtfully made to suction onto any flat surface, such as the dashboard of your spacecraft. So not only can you choose among dildos with names like Predator 1 and Damian, but you also can enjoy the company's line of anal probes (er, butt plugs), which look more like outer-space creatures and the probes you might find on an alien spacecraft, though in cheerful colors.

If your fantasies are more Earth-bound, but you're still curious about having fun with something other than the hominid-variety phallus, then the thoughtful kinksters at Zetacreations (zoofur.com) might have something to satisfy any zoological research you have in mind. This online store specializes in various silicone dildos shaped like animal penises (in addition to a selection of extra-large human models and gigantic nonrepresentational insertables). Size is indeed the name of the game at Zetacreations, where you won't find anything small, but rather items more along the lines of bears, marine mammals, and tigers.

And if you're not interested in human dildos, or bestial or alien ones, where else in the world of dildos and butt plugs can you possibly go? Into the realm of the spirit, of course. Divine Interventions (divine-interventions.com) might seem like several (web) pages out of the Book of Blasphemy, but this company is heaven-sent for those who like their finely crafted silicone dildos served up with a heaping slice of irony (and thought-fully designed for pleasure). The Baby Jesus Butt Plug is perhaps its best-known product, followed by the Jackhammer Jesus ("Jesus was a carpenter, now he's the powertool"), which is engi-neered to hit the G-spot with stunning accuracy. Christianity isn't the only religion on show here, since you can also find Buddha's Delight, though I'll wager that followers of Buddhism are less likely to get upset about where people choose to find their bliss.

Make Your Own Dildo

As it happens, if your imagination is so splendiferous that you don't care for *any* of the thousands of dildo types available from novelty companies, specialty boutiques, or even outer space, well, you can just make your own. Actually, the commercially avail-able make-it-yourself dildo, or Clone-A-Willy (cloneawilly.com), kits are sold with the idea that you have a penis at hand that you'd like to duplicate; for many couples, these kits present more than a few novel (and lightly kinky) ideas.

The kits sell for about a hundred dollars, and contain every-thing you need to make a dildo mold from a penis (or another dildo), plus the hygienic silicone for casting. Kits are also avail-able to cast your dildo in solid chocolate, for tasty eating later. With the silicone kits, casters get two cardboard cylinders, two bottles of powdered casting agent, a bottle of liquid silicone and activator, and a stick (to mix the silicone and activator, which will harden the silicone). Before casting, the man should coat his penis and pubic hair with Vaseline to make it easy to get the mold off him, and of course he'll also need an erection.

This process takes two people: one to mix the cold water and powdered mold-making mix, the other to help maintain the erection. Reason: When you mix the mold, it hardens within about two minutes, so the pressure on the model is high and the timing must be just right. That's why they provide you with two cylinders—two chances to get your timing right.

But after you mix the mold and plunge his penis into it, then wait for it to set (about 5 minutes), you can take your leisurely time mixing the silicone (or melting the chocolate) and pouring it into the mold—go slowly and be sure to tap out any air bubbles. Then, wait. In a couple of hours, the results are a stunning, lifelike cast of the penis, down to the veins, wrinkles, and all.

Chapter 9

Sex Furniture

If you could afford to have an extra room in your house devoted entirely to sexy things, or to have such a far-out, swinging pad that you could decorate it with sex toys as art, wouldn't you want to find a catalog that's the erotic version of Design Within Reach? Sadly, no such catalog exists, but online there are enough high-end artisan-crafted sex furniture sites to fill several pages of such a decadent directory. And, in practical terms, sex furniture offers better support for sex positions and play, can ease the strain of sex for people with injuries or limited mobility, and can make angling for G-spot and prostate stimulation easier.

Furniture Expressly for Sex

The LuvSeat (luvseat.com) is a sex chair available in three styles that incorporates a pneumatic spring and handlebars into an adjustable padded bench for all kinds of creative sex adventures. The website offers suggestions on positions and makes some

pretty outrageous claims about the chair curing premature ejaculation (your mileage may vary), but the sturdy, well-made,
attractive chair offers a lot for people who want to play on a
solid piece of sex furniture that offers many adjustable options.
Each LuvSeat holds up to 500 pounds; comes in black or bur-
gundy padded "ultra vinyl"; has optional foot stirrups, handles,
headrests, and seat covers, and comes with a five-year warranty.

Another seat-styled (and quite obvious) piece of sex furniture
is the Joy Rider (thejoyrider.com), a glossy black square-framed
chair that holds a suspended toilet seat. The uses for this sex
chair are left to your imagination, and while it's not sex-posi-
tion friendly for traditional penetration, it certainly looks like
it makes oral sex, BDSM, and helplessness predicaments very
intense. It's completely collapsible for discreet storage.

With its sleek polished wood base and sumptuous silk bro-
cade cushion, curved in a sexy sideways S, the Tantra Chair
(tantrachair.com) looks more a piece of antique Asian furniture
than a sex device—which is exactly what the designers had in
mind. While designed to accommodate the positions of the Kama
Sutra, the chair also doubles as a really beautiful living room
fixture that could easily pass for designer décor. Buyers decide
on the finishing details of each chair: It comes in a full range of
Thai silk brocades, cottons, or leather; and its base is made of
polished mahogany or maple (from sustainable forests). Each
chair has a five-year warranty.

Two absolutely stunning sex furniture designs can be found
at London-based Coco de Mer (coco-de-mer-shop.co.uk), most
notably the Poker Table and the Tally Ho Chair. Both look
straight out of a 1920s bordello (the really, really expensive kind)
and feature polished metal and padded black leather. No one

would know the extra use your Poker Table got up to after hours, unless they took a second look at the extra-sturdy, ornately shaped five-legged base and glossy black leather padded surface. But the Tally Ho Chair is another case entirely; it's impossible to think that even while someone might get caught up in admiring the beauty of its shape and sheen, they'd miss the equestrian shape, black leather leg stirrups, reins, and extra spanking (or kneeling) bench.

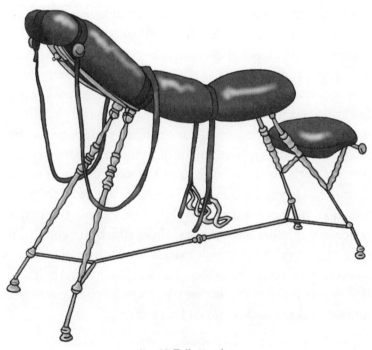

Illus. 16: Tally Ho Chair

Bondage Beds

If you really don't care who sees your kink, and can't suffer bad taste, treat yourself to a custom-made bondage bed from Dungeon Beds (dungeonbeds.com). These stunning steel creations cost a lot, but take a look at the quality, style, and options for kinky sex in a bed like the Dore Alley—a stark square shape with metal restraint hoops on all corners, crossbars for suspension, and votive candle lighting. The designers and fabricators behind Dungeon Beds have over a dozen years of furniture-making experience, and it shows in each of their incredible designs. But they haven't stopped with beds. The discriminating kinky decorator can also choose from bondage-friendly nightstands, bedside hanging shelves, and a steel cage dining table that allows you to lock a naughty someone in a cage beneath the dining table where you and dinner guests can take turns feeding or teasing the captive throughout your *very interesting* dinner party.

Can't spare the expense or flashiness of a Dore Alley bed, but still want to add more functionality to the bed you already have? A couple of companies make bondage bed sheets and bed straps that come out for a night of fun, then get washed and put discreetly away for future use. The most widely available, Sportsheets (sportsheets.com), offers a Bondage Bedsheets package that includes a fitted, velvet-like, Velcro-compatible bedcover with four anchor pads; these attach to Sports Cuffs to bind an arm or leg, which then can quickly be attached to an anchor pad on the bed sheet. The firm also has an Under The Bed kit, an under-mattress pad that includes cuffs and tethers for beds lacking anchor points for restraints.

Sex Slings and Swings

Weightless sex isn't just for naughty astronauts, swingers' conventions, or BDSM dungeons. Sex slings and swings are now widely available in adult stores and retail sites, and while all the usual cautions about quality should be mentioned, most models are durable, are of excellent quality, and can be relied on to hold a body (or even two) weightlessly while the players engage in any sex acts they can physically perform. They're also a boon for people with disabilities or limited mobility. Besides making the missionary position into a deliciously delightful experience where one partner can manipulate the other by effortlessly moving the swing or sling, these toys also make oral sex outrageous, doggy-style unbelievable, and activities like hand jobs and fisting simply incredible.

For ages, swings have been called *slings* by the BDSM community, but recently new types of suspension toys and haphazard naming practices among manufacturers have created a bit of confusion. Semantics aside, for our discussion a body harness is a specialized piece of nylon or leather that either acts as a sex position strap to keep part of the body aloft during penetration, or is sort of an adult carrying harness—acting like a sling. But in the world of sex toys, a sling is literally a swing that hangs suspended from the ceiling or a frame supplied by the manufacturer, so that a body can lie back in it and enjoy the ride. Typically, all swings and slings support up to 200 or even 400 pounds, but this differs between manufacturers and depends on how you set up your hangy thing.

The Body Swing is an inexpensive harness that straps to a man's body (or the person doing the penetrating); the penetratee sits up on the front of the wearer, fully supported by the harness. It has padded stirrups so the rider can get leverage, while the padded shoulder straps ease the strain on the harness wearer.

The Love Swing is an actual swing that hangs from a central connection point in a doorway frame or ceiling beam, and like most swings it comes with instructions for installation and investigating the load-bearing capacity of your hang points. (Its manufacturer wants you to play safely.) Here, you're basically hanging from and resting on straps. This swing's straps support the back and butt (or waist and knees) of the person in the swing. It also features padded stirrups for extra foot-ankle stability.

Classic slings hang from four points, but function like a swing and support the entire body with a piece of soft (yet thick) leather that the user can lie back on. Most have stirrups for feet or ankles, and many have rigging points for wrist bondage, so that the rider is flat on their back, weightless yet immobile. These are very expensive and can be hung from sturdy beams in a ceiling, or on sling stands that often cost the same as or more than the sling itself; you're paying for quality and options. Most steel bondage frames and sling stands are made of sturdy steel and bring with them a variety of suspension options besides using them with a sling (like upright flogging, suspension, vertical spread-eagle, and humiliation); they're usually easy to disassemble for storage.

Somewhere between a sex sling and sex furniture is the giddily named Bonk'er (bonkum.com), a set of standing suspension poles that curve into a heart shape over a bed, with rigging points for stirrups or a sling or both. The Bonk'er is sold in sets of two poles or four, is made of strong steel tubing and leather, and, according to its website, has been tested to withstand 350 pounds per set of two. It's sort of like having a trapeze set over your bed; users can lie back in it with legs held aloft, or a sling can be set up right over your bed. There are lots of possibilities here, and, should you run out of ideas, each set comes with a position guide booklet and a two-hour, explicit DVD demonstrating the Bonk'er in use. Some assembly is required.

Sex Position Pillows

While it's true that you can use any piece of furniture around your house to make a sex position more interesting or comfortable, you might not find your ottoman ideal for doggy-style, and a pile of pillows might make you feel more like the princess and the pea than a sex goddess. Especially when your pillows slip, or need to be readjusted when the going gets (nice and) rough. Sex position pillows are made expressly for sexual comfort and ease, and if you've never tried one, then you really don't know what you're missing.

The sex position pillows you'll want to look for are ones made of soft yet resilient foam, firm and with waterproof and removable (washable) covers. Knockoff companies will try to sell you poor imitations—inflatable pillows that will be cold and uncomfortable, will scratch on the plastic seams, are defective and leak air, or will pop before you do. Not to say that a Pilates ball isn't an excellent sex position toy—and it is, especially for oral sex.

The cream of the crop in sex position pillows is a brand called Liberator (liberatorshapes.com). Not only are the products stylish and thoughtfully designed, but the company came up with a stunning variety of props, pillows, and chaise-style furniture and accessories to make sex positions easier on everyone. This is especially good news for people with mobility issues. For instance, the Wedge and the Ramp are designed for use alone or in tandem to provide surfaces that make penetration easier and deeper, or to elevate the hips for intense G-spot stimulation or comfortable doggy-style penetration. Other models like the Esse are created with Kama Sutra positions in mind, and all their products come with full-color brochures with tasteful photographs of positions to use with the new purchase. Of course, a look at Liberator's clean, simple website will give you plenty of ideas all on your own (such as how to reproduce the pillows and positions at home, yourself). Their products aren't cheap—expect to start by spending at least two hundred dollars on a single pillow. But the waterproofing and removable covers are a nice touch.

Monkey Rocker

The Monkey Rocker (monkeyrocker.com) is essentially a non-mechanized sex machine, which sounds like an oxymoron until you understand that it's essentially an ingenious sex toy powered by the user's own body. It looks like a gorgeous Art Deco chair with the center of the seat missing; you sit comfortably on a padded, curved seat with a swing-arm dildo that rises in the center to meet your genitals when you rock back and forth on the highly stylish framework. The user controls the speed and motion absolutely, hands-free, and silently (well, at least the machine will remain quiet during the ride, even if you don't).

The way it works is that the user sits on the seat above the dildo; then they rock the hips back and forth (with feet on the floor), and as they move back and forth the dildo rises up and down, in and out. There's a curved handle on the front for the user's added stability if he or she needs to hold onto something besides their lover during the ride. In many ways, this is the perfect sex machine, as the user controls the rhythm, speed, and depth of penetration simply by rocking his or her hips, making for a totally customizable penetration experience—you get just what you want or need, when you need it the most.

The Monkey Rocker is like a pretty piece of furniture, yet weighs less than a Deco chair—at 25 pounds, it's relatively light-weight for its size. It's glossy and sleek looking, and comes in a huge variety of colors that can be mixed and customized to fit your décor. You can trick it out with the available high-end custom exotic veneers and personalized leather seat choices.

The makers of the Monkey Rocker want consumers to be able to use any toy they want with their machine, making it the most user-friendly sex machine available. When ordering, a shopper has two choices: either a Doc Johnson Vac-U-Lock system for dildo attachment (not out of any alliance with the toy manu-facturer, I learned, but simply from reasoning that Monkey Rocker wanted users to be able to easily find dildos for the machine) or a hard rubber strap and O-ring combination, making it easy to attach any flared-base sex toy to the machine.

The Doc Johnson Vac-U-Lock system enables users to apply any of that novelty manufacturer's toys to the Monkey Rocker, so if you have a lot of these toys lying around, there's no need to buy new toys for your new sex machine.

The strap and O-ring combination is the most versatile choice; with the strap and three different sized O-rings, users can enjoy any dildo they prefer, or, better yet, can even add a vibrating dildo. Vibrating silicone dildos! A range of sizes! This means that you pick the size, shape, and material for the dildo you want to use; this is the only sex machine that can be used interchangeably with literally any dildo (or butt plug, for that matter), including easy-to-clean, completely hygienic silicone toys. The O-ring system works well, and provides a very stable base for any dildo put in the straps.

This nonmechanical sex machine chair, to put it simply, provides hours of fun, whether alone or with a lover. It's easy to ride while watching porn (plus your hands are free for the fast-forward button, or the mouse). It's a great way to live out or simulate fantasies about double penetration, or just to enjoy penetration while providing oral sex. A woman could fuck herself silly while giving a blow job; conversely, a male rider could receive anal penetration while performing cunnilingus on a standing partner (or give a blow job to her strap-on cock).

Chapter 10

Shop Smart and Recommended Resources

Shopping for sex toys is an experience that can go one of two ways—toward delicious, rapturous success; or toward frustration and irritation at an industry that still thinks it sells "marital aids." Deciding what you want is one thing, finding it is another, and shopping smart is essential. As mentioned in the first chapter, some sex toys are poorly made, some retailers don't care if you get a broken toy, and every online shopper needs to be careful about privacy issues—because even if your credit card is insured against fraud and the site uses a secure ordering database, you'll still need to make sure you don't get on an unwanted email list or are otherwise violated in the process.

Finding the toy you want takes first having an idea of what you might be looking for (or actually looking to do), then finding a place that has your item. It's important to determine your intentions in advance; know what you'd like your toy to do, and have a specific item or toy type in mind. Or if you just want a little inspiration, browse through a retailer's toys (a fun game for couples to play), whether online or at a physical store.

Couples who shop together sometimes have as much fun selecting sex toys as they do using them, and even the online ordering process might result in a quickie at the computer. But what's really great about shopping for sex toys together is the learning experience—here, you get to ask your lover naughty questions about things they'd like to try, and in the bargain you learn a lot about their fantasies and how to please them in the process, as they do about you.

The other half of the equation is finding a good place to shop, though unfortunately most stores have agreements with distributors or manufacturers that make it tough for a consumer to find all the toys they want at only one store. So if you have a fantasy scene in mind, or have envisioned the "just right" toy combination for your fantasy weekend, be prepared to shop at more than one store. Of course, you can do a lot of your shopping at one site, amazon.com (whose prices are usually rock-bottom), but that has its disadvantages, too, as you'll still have your items shipped from different warehouses within the Amazon empire (meaning various arrival times for your packages), and the quality will vary greatly from store to store. And don't expect these stores to have great return policies on broken items—it's a risk.

If you're shopping in a real, in-person store, it should be a comfortable place to shop. Almost all major cities have a selection of adult toy, book, and video shops that are somewhat (or even very) sleazy and uncomfortable to shop in, generally because they aren't clean or kept up in any visible way, and the customers and clerks don't seem to want to be there. While these can be a taste of pure adventure for couples, keep in mind that you'll likely see things in the store that'll totally turn you off or offend you—or will make you run from the store laughing. Often, though, these stores are not so scary and you'll get what you want, pay the bored cashier (who's seen it all, by the way), and go home to get it on and get off with your new toys. Either way, it's highly recommended that, before you buy anything online or in person, you make the trek to a store so that you can see and handle the toys in person at least once, giving you both a realistic idea of what you're buying (or not).

Woman-oriented sex toy boutiques are styled specifically toward couples and single women. You'll see a lot of other women (and men) shopping there—people of every stripe and persuasion, having fun buying vibrators and cock rings. Unfortunately these clean, well-lit places to shop for sex toys are found in only a few major cities (see resource lists in the next section).

Many people choose to buy their products online. The privacy that the Web affords has made it both easy and safe for everyone to try out new sexual ideas and explore new possibilities, and it puts sex toys within everyone's geographic reach. However, the Internet can be dicey if you don't know the company's privacy policy (some companies sell your information to other parties), and it's difficult to ask questions about the products, unless the company provides an information phone line on their site.

On websites, it's vital that you safeguard your privacy. Shop at only reputable online stores; if you're not sure about their reputation, see if they have online forums where you can garner customer feedback, or check to see if they have actual brick-and-mortar stores (a sign of stability), or Google their URL and name to see what you dig up. Look into their privacy policy—if it's dodgy, shop elsewhere. See how they ship their products—is it done discreetly, and do the toys come in plain packages? And finally, see how their products are presented—if they have offensive or misspelled product descriptions or sell products that are unsafe, or if they just seem a bit off, then they'll likely treat their customers with the same disdain. Do they have annoying pop-up windows when you're trying to shop? Skip 'em. Shop with a company you like (vote with your credit card!), and if that company has an educational section or mission, even better.

Online Shopping, U.S.

Adam and Eve: adameve.com
A Woman's Touch: a-womans-touch.com (retail store in Madison)
Babeland: babeland.com (retail stores in Seattle and New York)
Blowfish: blowfish.com
Eve's Garden: evesgarden.com (retail store in New York)
Extreme Restraints: extremerestraints.com
Fatale Media: fatalemedia.com (for the film *Bend Over Boyfriend* and other great sex how-to videos)
Forbidden Fruit: forbiddenfruit.com (retail store in Austin)
Good Vibrations: goodvibes.com (retail stores in San Francisco, Oakland, Berkeley, and Brookline, MA)
Hidden Self: hiddenself.com
Hustler Hollywood: hustlerhollywood.com (retail stores in West Hollywood, San Diego, Ft. Lauderdale, Lexington, New Orleans, Berkeley, MO, Las Vegas, Monroe, OH, Columbus, Cincinnati, Nashville, and Tacoma)
JT's Stockroom: stockroom.com
Libida: libida.com
My Pleasure: mypleasure.com

Pleasure Chest: thepleasurechest.com (retail stores in New York, Los Angeles, and Chicago)

Purple Passion: purplepassion.com

Sportsheets: sportsheets.com

Tantus Silicone: tantussilicone.com (silicone toys; the Feeldoe)

Vixen Creations: vixencreations.com (silicone toys; Nexus, Nexus Jr., VixSkin)

Xandria: xandria.com

Online Shopping, Canada

Come As You Are: comeasyouare.com (retail store in Toronto)

Good For Her: goodforher.com (retail store in Toronto)

Lovecraft: lovecraftsexshop.com (retail store in Mississauga)

Womyn's Ware: womynsware.com (retail store in Vancouver)

Online Shopping, U.K.

Ann Summers: annsummers.com

Babes 'N Horny: babes-n-horny.com

Blissbox: blissbox.com

Cliterati: cliterati.co.uk

Coco de Mer: coco-de-mer.com (retail store in Covent Garden, London)

LoveHoney: lovehoney.co.uk

Myla: myla.com (retail store in London)

Sh! Women's Erotic Emporium: sh-womenstore.com (retail store in Hoxton Square, London)

Taboo: taboo.co.uk

Online Shopping, Australia and New Zealand

Bliss for Women: bliss4women.com (retail store in Melbourne)

D.vice: dvice.co.nz (retail stores in Auckland, Wellington, and Palmerston North)

Femplay: femplay.com.au

Ms. Naughty's For the Girls Superstore: msnaughty.inadult.com

Online Shopping, Europe

Blissbox: blissbox.com (sites for shipping to Netherlands, Germany, and Belgium)

Concorde Boutique: concorde.fr (retail store in Paris)

Demonia: boutique.demonia.com (retail store in Paris)

Senkys: senkys.com (France)

Voissa: voissa.com (France)

Sex Machines

Fucking Machines: fuckingmachines.com (not a retail site)

Ken's Twisted Mind: kenstwistedmind.com

Monkey Rocker: monkeyrocker.com

Orgasm Alley: orgasmalley.com

Sybian: sybian.com

Thethrillhammer: dnn.thethrillhammer.com

Teledildonics

High Joy: highjoy.com
Slashdong: slashdong.org

Exotic Sex Toys

Alien Dildos: aliendildos.com
Clone-A-Willy: cloneawilly.com
Coco de Mer: coco-de-mer.com
Divine Interventions: divine-interventions.com
Elemental Pleasures: elementalpleasures.com
Je Joue Programmable Vibrator: jejoue.com
Lelo: lelo.com
Njoy Toys: njoytoys.com
Shiri Zinn's Minx Vibrator: shirizinn.com
Zetacreations: zoofur.com

Sex Furniture

Bonk'er: bonkum.com
Coco de Mer: coco-de-mer.com
Dungeon Beds: dungeonbeds.com
Joy Rider: thejoyrider.com

JT's Stockroom: stockroom.com (swings and slings)
Liberator: liberator.com
Monkey Rocker: monkeyrocker.com
Tantra Chair: tantrachair.com

Highly Recommended Reading

Come Hither: A Common Sense Guide to Kinky Sex, by Gloria Brame
Exhibitionism for the Shy: Show Off, Dress Up and Talk Hot, by Carol Queen
Family Jewels: A Guide to Male Genital Play and Torment, by Hardy Haberman
The Guide to Getting It On!, by Paul Joannides
Healing Sex: A Mind-Body Approach to Healing Sexual Trauma, by Staci Haines
The Mistress Manual, by Mistress Lorelei
Sensuous Magic: A Guide to S/M for Adventurous Couples, by Patrick Califia
Sex Toys 101, by Rachel Venning and Claire Cavanah
The Stripper's Guide to Looking Great Naked, by Jennifer Axen and Leigh Phillips
Sweet Life: Erotic Fantasies for Couples 1 and *2*, and *Sweet Danger*, by Violet Blue
The Toybag Guides, Greenery Press, by various authors
Tricks...to Please a Man, by Jay Wiseman
Tricks...to Please a Woman, by Jay Wiseman
The Ultimate Guide to Anal Sex for Women, by Tristan Taormino
The Ultimate Guide to Orgasm for Women, by Mikaya Heart
The Ultimate Guide to Sex and Disability, by Miriam Kaufman, MD, Cory Silverberg, and Fran Odette

The Ultimate Guide to Sexual Fantasy, by Violet Blue
The Ultimate Guide to Strap-On Sex, by Karlyn Lotney
When the Earth Moves: Women and Orgasm, by Mikaya Hart

Safer Sex Information

Before you put each other's naughty bits in your mouths, or even think about rubbing your bodies together, it's a good idea to know where these bits have been. But since we don't all live in a perfect world—in fact, no one does—you'll want to use condoms, gloves, dental dams, or finger cots when you have oral, vaginal, or anal sex; when you use or share sex toys; and, in some cases, when you give hand jobs. When someone pulls out a condom, dam, glove, or cot, you know you're literally in good hands. Below is a list of items in your first line of defense against invading infections and viruses:

Condoms: Available in latex and polyurethane, in dozens of sizes, colors, and flavors. Animal skin condoms don't prevent the spread of some viruses. A condom is a snug sheath that unrolls onto a penis or sex toy. Use condoms for fellatio, for vaginal and anal sex, and for covering sex toys made of porous materials, or when you want to share a sex toy. Change condoms for different sex partners and orifices—something that has been used anally should be covered by a condom before it's inserted orally or vaginally. Don't reuse your toy condoms. Don't use anything containing oils of any kind that latex condoms may come in contact with; however, polyurethane condoms may be used with oils.

Dental dams: Thin squares of latex or polyurethane used as a barrier for cunnilingus and rimming. Lubricate the genitals, place the dam on top, keep a good hold on the dam, and lick to your heart's content. Available in a few flavors and colors; in a jam, you can use plastic wrap or a condom cut open and laid flat.

Gloves: Use latex or nonlatex gloves for hand jobs on persons of all genders. They protect against germs from your hands going onto genitals, can protect your hands from picking up viruses or germs, and make hands a smooth surface free of jagged nails or scratchy calluses.

Finger cots: Tiny condoms made of latex that unroll over a finger to create a sterile surface. Great for on-the-go escapades.

If you choose to go at it uncovered, here is what you're at risk for. Make an informed decision!

Sharing Sex Toys

HIGH RISK	MODERATE RISK	NO RISK	N/A
Chlamydia	Bacterial vaginosis	None	None
Gonorrhea	Hepatitis A		
Hepatitis B	Hepatitis C		
HIV	Herpes		
Syphilis	HPV		
	Lice/scabies		
	Vaginitis		

Anal to Oral Contact (Penis or Sex Toy)

HIGH RISK	MODERATE RISK	NO RISK	N/A
Gonorrhea	Chlamydia	Lice/scabies	Bacterial vaginosis
Hepatitis A	Hepatitis C		Vaginitis
Hepatitis B	HIV		
Herpes			
HPV			
Syphilis			

Unprotected Anal to Vaginal Contact

HIGH RISK	MODERATE RISK	NO RISK	N/A
Bacterial vaginosis	Hepatitis C		Lice/scabies
Chlamydia			
Gonorrhea			
Hepatitis A			
Hepatitis B			
Herpes			
HIV			
HPV			
Syphilis			

About the Author

VIOLET BLUE (tinynibbles.com, @violet blue, about.me/ violetblue) is an award-winning author and editor, CNET reporter, CBSi/ZDNet blogger and columnist, a high-profile tech personality and one of *Wired*'s Faces of Innovation. She is regarded as the foremost expert in the field of sex and technology, a sex-positive mainstream media pundit (*MacLife*, CNN, "The Oprah Winfrey Show") and is interviewed, quoted and featured in outlets ranging from ABC News to the *Wall Street Journal*.

Blue was the notorious sex columnist for the *San Francisco Chronicle*. She has been at the center of many Internet scandals, including Google's "nymwars" and Libya's web domain censorship and seizures—*Forbes* calls her "omnipresent on the web" and named her a Forbes Web Celeb. She headlines and keynotes at global technology conferences including ETech, LeWeb, SXSW: Interactive and two Google Tech Talks at Google, Inc. and received a standing ovation at Seattle's Gnomedex.

The *London Times* named Violet Blue "one of the 40 bloggers who really count."

Classic Sex Guides

The Smart Girl's Guide to the G-Spot
Violet Blue

It's not a myth, it's a miracle, the G-spot, that powerhouse of female orgasm. With wit and panache, sex educator and bestselling writer Violet Blue helps readers master the sexual alphabet through G.
ISBN 978-1-57344-780-5 $14.95

The Smart Girl's Guide to Porn
Violet Blue

As seen on the Oprah Winfrey show!
Looking for authentic sex scenes? Thinking of sharing porn with a lover? Wonder which browser is safest for Internet porn surfing? *The Smart Girl's Guide to Porn* has the answers.
ISBN 978-1-57344-247-3 $14.95

The Adventurous Couple's Guide to Sex Toys
Violet Blue

Feeling adventurous? In this witty and well-informed consumer guide, bestselling author and sex educator Violet Blue shows couples how to choose and use sex toys to play and explore together—and have mind-blowing sex.
ISBN 978-1-57344-972-4 $14.95

The Adventurous Couple's Guide to Strap-On Sex
Violet Blue

"If you're seriously considering making it a part of your sexual repertoire, *The Adventurous Couple's Guide to Strap-On Sex* will give you all the advice you need to enjoy it in a safe and satisfying fashion" —*Forum UK*
ISBN 978-1-57344-278-7 $14.95

Seal It With a Kiss
Violet Blue

A great kiss can stop traffic, start a five-alarm fire, and feel like Times Square on New Year's Eve. Get your smooch on with all the different tricks and tips found in *Seal It with a Kiss*.
ISBN 978-1-57344-385-2 $12.95

THE ULTIMATE GUIDES

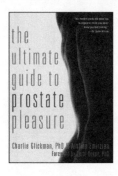

"Vanillas, novices, old hands, old guard—everyone can learn from this collection."

—Dan Savage

The Ultimate Guide to Prostate Pleasure
Erotic Exploration for Men and Their Partners

Charlie Glickman, PhD and Aislinn Emirzian

$17.95, 6" x 9", 368 Pages,
Health/Sexuality,
ISBN: 978-1-57344-904-5,
Trade Paper, 32/case,
Rights: World

The Ultimate Guide to Kink
BDSM, Role Play and the Erotic Edge

Tristan Taormino

$19.95, 6" x 9", 464 Pages,
Sexuality,
ISBN: 978-1-57344-779-9,
Trade Paper, 28/case,
Rights: World

The Ultimate Guide to Orgasm for Women
How to Become Orgasmic for a Lifetime

Mikaya Heart

$17.95, 6" x 9", 272 Pages,
Health/Sexuality,
ISBN: 978-1-57344-711-9,
Trade Paper, 40/case,
Rights: World

The Ultimate Guide to Cunnilingus
How to Go Down on a Woman and Give Her Exquisite Pleasure

Violet Blue

$16.95, 6" x 9", 200 Pages,
Sexuality,
ISBN: 978-1-57344-387-6,
Trade Paper, 52/case,
Rights: World

The Ultimate Guide to Fellatio
How to Go Down on a Man and Give Him Mind-Blowing Pleasure

Violet Blue

$16.95, 6" x 9", 272 Pages,
Sexuality,
ISBN: 978-1-57344-398-2,
Trade Paper, 36/case,
Rights: World

THE ULTIMATE GUIDES

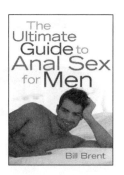

The Ultimate Guide to Anal Sex for Women

Tristan Taormino

$16.95, 6" x 9", 240 Pages,
Sexuality,
ISBN: 978-1-57344-221-3,
Trade Paper, 40/case,
Rights: World

The Ultimate Guide to Pregnancy for Lesbians
How to Stay Sane and Care for Yourself from Pre-conception Through Birth

Rachel Pepper

$17.95, 6" x 9", 288 Pages,
Health/Pregnancy & Childbirth,
ISBN: 978-1-57344-216-9,
Trade Paper, 36/case,
Rights: World

The Ultimate Guide to Anal Sex for Men

Bill Brent

$16.95, 6" x 9", 272 Pages,
Sexuality,
ISBN: 978-1-57344-121-6,
Trade Paper, 36/case,
Rights: World

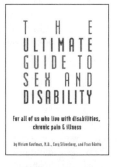

The Ultimate Guide to Sexual Fantasy
How to Turn Your Fantasies into Reality

Violet Blue

$15.95, 6" x 9", 272 Pages,
Sexuality,
ISBN: 978-1-57344-190-2,
Trade Paper, 32/case,
Rights: World

The Ultimate Guide to Sex and Disability
For All of Us Who Live with Disabilities, Chronic Pain and Illness

Miriam Kaufman, M.D., Cory Silverberg and Fran Odette

$18.95, 6" x 9", 360 Pages,
Health/Sexuality,
ISBN: 978-1-57344-304-3,
Trade Paper, 24/case,
Rights: World

"A welcome resource.... This book will be a worthwhile read for anyone who lives with a disability, loves someone with a disability, or simply wants to be better informed sexually."
—Curve

Bestselling Erotica for Couples

Sweet Life
Erotic Fantasies for Couples
Edited by Violet Blue

Your ticket to a front row seat for first-time spankings, breathtaking role-playing scenes, sex parties, women who strap it on and men who love to take it, not to mention threesomes of every combination.
ISBN 978-1-57344-133-9 $14.95

Sweet Life 2
Erotic Fantasies for Couples
Edited by Violet Blue

"This is a we-did-it-you-can-too anthology of real couples playing out their fantasies." —Lou Paget, author of *365 Days of Sensational Sex*
ISBN 978-1-57344-167-4 $15.95

Sweet Love
Erotic Fantasies for Couples
Edited by Violet Blue

"If you ever get a chance to try out your number-one fantasies in real life—and I assure you, there will be more than one—say yes. It's well worth it. May this book, its adventurous authors, and the daring and satisfied characters be your guiding inspiration."—Violet Blue
ISBN 978-1-57344-381-4 $14.95

Afternoon Delight
Erotica for Couples
Edited by Alison Tyler

"Alison Tyler evokes a world of heady sensuality where fantasies are fearlessly explored and dreams gloriously realized."
—Barbara Pizio, Executive Editor, *Penthouse Variations*
ISBN 978-1-57344-341-8 $14.95

Three-Way
Erotic Stories
Edited by Alison Tyler

"Three means more of everything. Maybe I'm greedy, but when it comes to sex, I like more. More fingers. More tongues. More limbs. More tangling and wrestling on the mattress."
ISBN 978-1-57344-193-3 $15.95

Many More Than Fifty Shades of Erotica

Please, Sir
Erotic Stories of Female Submission
Edited by Rachel Kramer Bussel

If you liked *Fifty Shades of Grey*, you'll love the explosive stories of *Yes, Sir*. These damsels delight in the pleasures of taking risks to be rewarded by the men who know their deepest desires. Find out why nothing is as hot as the power of the words "Please, Sir."
ISBN 978-1-57344-389-0 $14.95

Yes, Sir
Erotic Stories of Female Submission
Edited by Rachel Kramer Bussel

Bound, gagged or spanked—or controlled with just a glance—these lucky women experience the breathtaking thrills of sexual submission. *Yes, Sir* shows that pleasure is best when dispensed by a firm hand.
ISBN 978-1-57344-310-4 $15.95

He's on Top
Erotic Stories of Male Dominance and Female Submission
Edited by Rachel Kramer Bussel

As true tops, the bossy hunks in these stories understand that BDSM is about exulting in power that is freely yielded. These kinky stories celebrate women who know exactly what they want.
ISBN 978-1-57344-270-1 $14.95

Best Bondage Erotica 2012
Edited by Rachel Kramer Bussel

How do you want to be teased, tied and tantalized? Whether you prefer a tough top with shiny handcuffs, the tug of rope on your skin or the sound of your lover's command, Rachel Kramer Bussel serves your needs.
ISBN 978-1-57344-754-6 $15.95

Luscious
Stories of Anal Eroticism
Edited by Alison Tyler

Discover all the erotic possibilities that exist between the sheets and between the cheeks in this daring collection. "Alison Tyler is an author to rely on for steamy, sexy page turners! Try her!"—Powell's Books
ISBN 978-1-57344-760-7 $15.95

Best Erotica Series

"Gets racier every year."—*San Francisco Bay Guardian*

Best Women's Erotica 2012
Edited by Violet Blue
ISBN 978-1-57344-755-3 $15.95

Best Women's Erotica 2011
Edited by Violet Blue
ISBN 978-1-57344-423-1 $15.95

Best Women's Erotica 2010
Edited by Violet Blue
ISBN 978-1-57344-373-9 $15.95

Best Bondage Erotica 2012
Edited by Rachel Kramer Bussel
ISBN 978-1-57344-754-6 $15.95

Best Bondage Erotica 2011
Edited by Rachel Kramer Bussel
ISBN 978-1-57344-426-2 $15.95

Best Fetish Erotica
Edited by Cara Bruce
ISBN 978-1-57344-355-5 $15.95

Best Lesbian Erotica 2012
Edited by Kathleen Warnock. Selected and
introduced by Sinclair Sexsmith.
ISBN 978-1-57344-752-2 $15.95

Best Lesbian Erotica 2011
Edited by Kathleen Warnock.
Selected and introduced by Lea DeLaria.
ISBN 978-1-57344-425-5 $15.95

Best Lesbian Erotica 2010
Edited by Kathleen Warnock.
Selected and introduced by BETTY.
ISBN 978-1-57344-375-3 $15.95

Best Gay Erotica 2012
Edited by Richard Labonté. Selected and
introduced by Larry Duplechan.
ISBN 978-1-57344-753-9, $15.95

Best Gay Erotica 2011
Edited by Richard Labonté.
Selected and introduced by Kevin Killian.
ISBN 978-1-57344-424-8 $15.95

Best Gay Erotica 2010
Edited by Richard Labonté. Selected and
introduced by Blair Mastbaum.
ISBN 978-1-57344-374-6 $15.95

In Sleeping Beauty's Bed
Erotic Fairy Tales
By Mitzi Szereto
ISBN 978-1-57344-367-8 $16.95

Can't Help the Way That I Feel
Sultry Stories of African American Love
Edited by Lori Bryant-Woolridge
ISBN 978-1-57344-386-9 $14.95

Making the Hook-Up
Edgy Sex with Soul
Edited by Cole Riley
ISBN 978-1-57344-3838 $14.95

* **Free book of equal or lesser value. Shipping and applicable sales tax extra.**
Cleis Press • (800) 780-2279 • orders@cleispress.com
www.cleispress.com

More Women's Erotica from Violet Blue

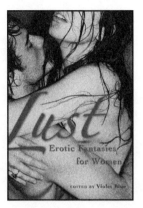

Ordering is easy! Call us toll free or fax us to place your MC/VISA order.
You can also mail the order form below with payment to:
Cleis Press, 2246 Sixth St., Berkeley, CA 94710.

ORDER FORM

QTY	TITLE	PRICE
_____	_____	_____
_____	_____	_____
_____	_____	_____
_____	_____	_____
_____	_____	_____
_____	_____	_____
_____	_____	_____
_____	_____	_____

	SUBTOTAL	_____
	SHIPPING	_____
	SALES TAX	_____
	TOTAL	_____

Add $3.95 postage/handling for the first book ordered and $1.00 for each additional book. Outside North America, please contact us for shipping rates. California residents add 9% sales tax. Payment in U.S. dollars only.

★ Free book of equal or lesser value. Shipping and applicable sales tax extra.

Cleis Press • Phone: (800) 780-2279 • Fax: (510) 845-8001
orders@cleispress.com • www.cleispress.com
You'll find more great books on our website

Follow us on Twitter @cleispress • Friend/fan us on Facebook